British Teenage Dolls 1956–1984

British Teenage Dolls 1956–1984

New Cavendish Books
London

First published in the UK by New Cavendish Books

Publisher: Narisa Chakra
Design: Olivia Koerfer

ISBN: 1 872727 46 8

New Cavendish Books
3 Denbigh Road
London W11 2SJ
Tel: 020 7229 6765
Fax: 020 7792 0027
email: narisa@dircon.co.uk
www.newcavendishbooks.co.uk

Printed and bound in Thailand by Amarin Printing & Publishing [Plc] Co. Ltd.

CONTENTS

ACKNOWLEDGEMENTS

Special thanks to my sons Simon and Julian Baird for loaning part of their collection of Action Man to be photographed. To my husband Peter for his invaluable contribution. To Christopher Wimsey, Rosemary Palmer and Margaret Williams for their help searching for doll models and clothes. Last but not least the retired manufacturers that replied to my correspondence, phone calls and questions.

All the dolls illustrated are from the Author's collection unless otherwise stated.

Photography by Colin W. D. P. Greene

Having spent several decades collecting my favourite childhood hard plastic dolls from the early post-war years, I came across these smaller, slim teenage dolls by chance after listening to office colleagues discussing their daughters' favourite toys. One mother was evidently 'for' and the other definitely 'against' these new dolls. Boxed in their unmentionables (bra, panties, stockings), these 'sexy' new adult-figured dolls with uplifted busts and cleavage had quickly developed a devoted following among young girls. Parents of the late Fifties were horrified to see dolls dressed in such realistic, provocative underwear, and to realise that their daughters wanted one for Christmas was rather a shock to the system. Realism was what children wanted, however, and this type of doll has stood the test of time; today, they are as popular as ever, after more than forty years in the toy shops.

On checking out this phenomenon known as 'the teenage doll', I found that they it was far more interesting than I at first envisaged. These dolls came superbly dressed, with a range of fashion clothes and accessories (available separately) that any teenager would envy – and all at pocket-money prices that the child could save for, collect and aspire to. Many new teenage dolls have appeared over the years and several models have been based on a family theme, with family members, partners and friends to collect, many of them with individual, characters and names. Times change, though, and as each generation likes to be different from the last, so, too, the dolls have changed – from 'family' oriented characters to 'career girls', 'pop singers' and 'super stars'.

This book depicts the most popular of the British teenage dolls (there were many others produced in the U.S.A., Europe and Australia) – from the larger models (15"-24", 38cm-61cm) of the late Fifties through to the smaller dolls (6"-12"/15cm-31cm) of the Sixties and Seventies. It also includes a wide variety of fashion clothes and accessories available for each named doll: the Fifties produced circular skirts and sweaters, the Sixties mini skirts and hot-pants, the Seventies wild Flower-Power flared trousers and long coats, and the Eighties sporty casual and career-girl glamour. In the 'teenage doll', the doll enthusiast has more than forty years of fashion to collect.

Teenage dolls were first introduced to the market in the late Fifties, in sizes between 10"/26cm and 24"/61cm. Now that the postwar baby boomers were growing up into the first pre-teens and teenagers, the doll manufacturers wanted to acknowledge this new group with dolls to match their lifestyle, with fashionable clothes, boyfriends and, later, cars, room-settings and homes. These dolls were made from a soft plastic called vinyl, a mixture of poly-vinyl-chloride and polythene that could be blow-moulded cheaply and could accommodate rooted hair (rather than having a glued-on wig). These early teenage dolls were not ultra slim like the later Barbie, Sindy and Tressy dolls, but just a shapelier version of the conventional fashion-girl dolls of the time. They were made by most of the British manufacturers, who withdrew many of their hard plastic dolls following the introduction of the new, softer vinyl material.

At first these 'British' dolls were made in Britain, but by the mid-Sixties production of most had been moved to Hong Kong, where labour was much cheaper. The dolls were marketed as having shapely limbs and uplifted busts with cleavage, twist waists and arched feet to enable them to wear high-heeled sandals. They had five basic joints that moved: head, arms and legs. Their faces were painted with make-up and their fingers and toes with nail varnish. They were packaged wearing either their lingerie (bra, panties, stockings) and high heeled shoes or sandals, or sophisticated evening dresses, strapless day dresses, bridal wear or beachwear, and each outfit came with matching shoes or sandals and items of jewellery such as necklaces, earrings, rings and bangles. Although clothes were produced separately for these dolls in the early Sixties under such names as Mamselle, Amanda Jane, Faerie Glen and others, it was still the norm to dress a doll oneself from dressmaking and knitting patterns available in women's magazines.

If you were born in the Forties or Fifties you will almost certainly identify with the fashions these dolls were wearing and will probably be thinking: 'I wore a dress just like that when I was 18' or, as a friend exclaimed to me, 'I was married in that style of bridal gown in 1951!' (doll fashions were always a few years behind reality in those days). Companies copied one another; many of these larger teenage dolls were similar in appearance, with a short bubble-cut hairstyle and a circular skirt worn with a sweater, reminiscent of the fashions of the late Fifties.

The teenage doll had really taken off by 1959 and was popular enough for manufacturers in the U.S.A. to introduce a 12"/30cm model that could more easily be carried about by a child. Indeed, small, com-partmentalised carry cases were produced so that a child could carry a doll and its accessories around with her wherever she went. Barbie, manufactured by Mattel in the U.S.A., was one of the first popular 12"/30cm, slimmer teenage dolls, introduced in 1959 with a separate wardrobe of fashion clothes reflecting the couture of the times. Young girls could learn about make-up, hairstyles, fashionable clothes and jewellery all through the one doll at a fairly affordable price – many outfits were geared to pocket-money prices and a fantastic wardrobe could be built up for a favourite doll over a year or two that reflected the child's own, or an older sibling's or mother's lifestyle, to which they aspired.

Mattel's Barbie became so popular that she revolutionised the doll scene completely. Other manufacturers quickly followed Mattel's lead, with dolls such as Tammy and Tressy. By the early Sixties, British manufacturers followed suit and introduced slim 12"/30cm teenage dolls, too. First came Sindy and friends, then a British version of Tressy and friends, followed by Tina, Action Girl, Pippa, Daisy and many more; some, like Tressy, were American-inspired, others were more home grown. Through television advertising in the early Sixties and Seventies these slim teenage dolls, their fashions and accessories were to become best sellers, turned out at the rate of 10,000 dolls a day; they have remained popular over the intervening forty-odd years, and today are produced in their millions. Children were also encouraged to collect additional dolls in the form of 'friends' and 'boyfriends' of the original doll as well as additional fashions for them, through tokens printed on the packaging – collect enough 'hearts', 'stars' or 'petals' and you could send off for a free gift, such as a nude doll. This book highlights the early and most popular of these British-made teenage dolls and shows their fashions and many accessories. Together they reflect very well the fashion and culture of the last forty years and they are now avidly sought not only by the doll collector, but also by the fashion enthusiast (who perhaps also remembers playing with them as a child).

The teenage doll reflects fashions from the era in which it was produced. The Fifties dolls have fashions from Hartnell and Vogue, with circular skirts, sweaters, two-piece suits and tiny accessories; the dolls of the Swinging Sixties have the Mod fashions of Mary Quant, with mini skirts and hot-pants and a leaning towards beautiful homes, room settings, furniture and kitchen gadgets. The bright hippie colours of the Seventies are represented in bell-bottom flared trousers and maxi skirts and coats while the Eighties fashions see a shift towards designer clothes and jewellery of the career girl or sports clothes and tracksuits of the keep-fit enthusiast.

In the early Sixties the teenage 'boyfriend' doll had been introduced in the U.S.A. in the form of Barbie's boyfriend Ken. Never before had this older type of male doll been produced; previously, dolls dressed as boys were seen as 'babies' or 'little brothers'. Again, British companies were quick to copy the trend and Sindy's boyfriend Paul was introduced in 1966, but had been dropped by the end of the Sixties as it seemed that little girls preferred to keep their teenage-girl dolls to themselves and not share them with a 'boyfriend'. Another kind of male doll was introduced in the U.S.A. in 1964. This was a doll for boys to play with and was dressed in military uniforms. He was called G.I. Joe. The British version, Action Man, appeared in 1966, and almost immediately he had a rival in Tommy Gunn. These soldier dolls proved to be very popular, but it was Action Man that won the sales ratings, and Tommy Gunn was discontinued after just over a year in production. Action Man went from strength to strength, however, and over the years his designers shifted from putting him in basic military uniform to presenting him in various outfits in themed series such as Soldiers of the World, Adventurers, Famous British Uniforms, Sportsmen, Wild West and Space Fantasy, to keep abreast of the times. Action Man was discontinued in 1984, after eighteen years in production, but was reintroduced in the Nineties.

I did not play with any of these teenage dolls myself as, by 1960, I was already leading the lifestyle that these teenage dolls portrayed. It was not until I started to collect these dolls, more than four decades ago, that I realised the attraction they had for pre-teen girls, who could copy their older sisters or their mothers through role-play. Now, of course, pure nostalgia is the attraction for the post-war baby boomers, who were teenagers in the late Fifties and Sixties – the make-up, the teenage fashions and the lifestyle, with coffee bars, rock'n'roll, Tommy Steele, Joe Brown, Marty Wilde, Billy Fury, Cliff Richards and Helen Shapiro. The clothes were wonderful for the girl fans, with full circular skirts and masses of tiered petticoats, earrings and jewellery, nylon stockings and strappy high-heeled shoes. So it is for anyone else who remembers and identifies with the fashion styles of the last fifty years.

Late 50s
and larger teenage dolls

While some of the earliest teenage dolls had individual names, these were for identification on the catalogue and for ease of ordering by the toy-shop retailers. During the late Fifties there was no television advertising for individual toys and children generally knew only the name of the company that made their doll (Palitoy, Pedigree, Roddy, Rosebud, etc.), not its catalogue name. It was usual, then, for children to give these dolls names of their own.

Made from a mix of the new soft vinyl plastic (poly-vinyl-chloride) and polythene, as adopted by most British manufacturers by 1957, the new teenage doll was slimmer and more shapely than previous dolls. Instead of being presented in traditional children's style party dresses and strap-style flat shoes, these dolls came wearing ladies 'undies' (bra, panties, stockings) and high-heeled sandals. Some also came ready dressed in the box, with additional boxed outfits available for them in the modern styles that little girls would have seen their teen sisters or mothers wearing. Never before had a mass-produced doll been dressed as a fashionable modern adult; previously, adult dolls had been dressed in national or historical costume.

One of the first of these teenage dolls was the 'Roddy' doll, designed and produced by D.G. Todd & Co in 1957, after a visit to its competitors in the U.S.A. to look at manufacturing techniques. Todd & Co's British competitors, anxious to attract sales in this new market, followed suit in the late 1950s and early 1960s with their own interpretations of the teenage doll. During these few years a wonderful array of larger teenage dolls emerged wearing everyday dresses, beauty-queen outfits, bridal gowns and attractive evening wear.

The most popular of these dolls came in 10"/26cm, 15"/38cm and 20"/51cm sizes, with a few at 24"/61cm. The dolls in this section are chronicled under their manufacturer's name.

CHILTERN (H.G. Stone & Co of Chesham)

This company introduced its first teenage dolls in 1958 in three sizes: 11"/28cm, 15"/38cm and 20"/51cm tall. The dolls had three different, rooted hairstyles: a short elfin cut, a longer wavy shoulder-length style and a long ponytail. All three styles came in blonde, fair and brunette – and a few dolls were given pale pink or pale blue hair. All of these hair types could be combed and shampooed. The Chiltern dolls had straight non-twist waists, five moveable joints (head, arms and hips), sleeping blue eyes, blue eye make-up, and red painted lips and finger- and toe-nails. Many had earrings and jewellery. Their feet were arched, which meant that their high-heeled white sandals would fit authentically. Some models were dressed only in white paper-nylon bra, panties and nylon stockings for dressing properly at home, others came in one of an array of fashion outfits.

The smallest of these dolls at 11"/28cm tall was the Ballerina doll. Although not dressed in a tutu, it did come dressed in a beautiful full-skirted knee-length dress of organdie, voil, brocade, satin, nylon and taffeta with a halter-neck, a velveteen cape and nylon undies, plus pearl earrings and white, strappy sandals. Most Ballerina dolls had the elfin haircut in blonde, fair or brunette, and one model had the pink or blue hair colour.

Just called 'teenage dolls', the 15"/38cm size Chiltern doll came with three hairstyles – elfin, wavy shoulder length and long ponytail – in blonde, fair, brunette, and pink or blue colours. This popular size of doll came dressed in a wide range of outfits: full skirted knee-length dresses in spotted, floral, tartan or check cottons with white pique collars; shiny cotton and nylon organza blouse and trousers, with one model in a red duffle coat; a longer-length evening dress of taffeta, nylon or rayon trimmed with pearls, pearl necklaces and earrings; a nylon nightdress and housecoat; and, last but not least, a bridal gown in layers of white nylon and net with a bouquet of flowers, and a pearl necklace and earrings. All outfits were worn with white high-heeled strappy sandals.

The 20"/51cm doll also came with the three hairstyles (elfin, wavy shoulder length and long ponytail) in blonde, fair, brunette, pink and blue. The clothes included knee-length day-time dresses with full skirts in spotted, floral and patterned cotton prints, with pique collars and reveres, and some had sewn on butterfly and flower motifs. There was also a pink-haired model that was especially pretty: it came in a pink, flocked nylon full-skirted party dress with tiered skirts and petticoats, with pearl necklace and earrings. Another model wore a stiffened cotton dress and jacket and yet another came in a yellow cotton spotted dress with matching sailcloth coat and hat; both were very chic. This 20"/51cm size also had a beautiful bride in white nylon, lace and net, wearing a headdress of pearls and pearl earrings, and carrying a bouquet of roses tied with ribbon. Madame Pompadour, another model in this size, came in a royal blue velvet cape and silver embroidered nylon dress with cuffs, and a specially styled ringlet hairdo. All these dolls came in white high-heeled strappy sandals.

The Chiltern teenage dolls were not individually named and the pink- and blue-haired models became very popular with children in the early Sixties and were copied by other manufacturers. These dolls were marked 'CHILTERN' (in capitals) and 'Made in England' across the back of the neck. The boxes were pink and blue card marked 'A Chiltern Doll' with white-hearts decoration.

Ballerina doll
Chiltern/H.G. Stone &
Co Ltd
11"/28cm
CHILTERN *Made in England* on the back of her neck
Early Sixties
The smallest of the family of teenage dolls made by this company, she is a fully jointed doll with arched feet. She has rooted short fair hair, blue sleeping eyes and painted finger and toe nails and is wearing her high-heeled sandals. Re-dressed.

Ballerina doll
Chiltern/H.G. Stone &
Co Ltd
11"/28cm
CHILTERN *Made in England* on the back of her neck
Early Sixties
As illustration (9), but wearing her original undies, stockings, sandals and black halter-neck ballerina length evening dress.

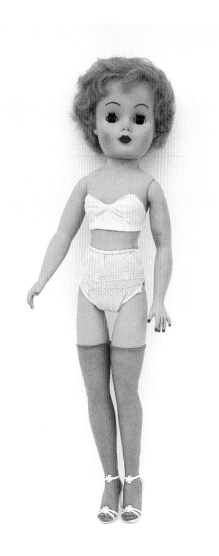

This illustration shows the trademark as it appears on the back of all Chiltern dolls.

Top left:
Teenage doll
Chiltern/H.G. Stone & Co Ltd
19"/48cm
CHILTERN Made in England on the back of her neck
1959
This lovely tall teenage doll was purchased in 1959. She has rooted fair curly nylon hair, sleeping blue eyes with blue eye shadow, painted red lips and painted finger and toe nails. She wears her original undies – bra, panties, nylons – and high-heeled sandals.

Top right:
Teenage doll
Chiltern/H.G. Stone & Co Ltd
15"/38cm
CHILTERN Made in England on the back of her neck
Early Sixties
Another Chiltern teenage doll. This one has rooted pale blonde hair, sleeping eyes with blue eye shadow, painted red lips and painted finger and toe nails. She wears her undies, stockings and a blue shimmery dress. Her heeled sandals are missing.

D.I.L. (Doll industries Ltd of North London)

This little-known company made vinyl teenage dolls that resembled the 'Roddy' when stripped of their clothing, as they had no maker's mark. (The company shared the same distributor as 'Roddy' from 1959 to the early 1970s.) It is only when a doll is found complete in its box that it can be attributed to Doll Industries Ltd. These were attractive dolls with rooted bubble-cut hairstyles in several colours. They had five moveable joints (head, arms and legs), sleeping blue eyes, lashes and painted lips, but no finger – or toe-nail paint. As with most other makes, the D.I.L. teenage dolls wore nylon bra and panties, nylon stockings and white high-heeled strappy sandals. The range included 15"/38cm and 21"/53cm dolls with dresses as varied as: a frilly, white and silver-sparkle fairy dress, cape and wand; a bride in creamy white satin and net; and a gala evening gown in pale satin, lace and ribbons. The dresses were beautifully made and trimmed in a wealth of sparkle, lace and satin ribbon. The boxes they came in were also particularly attractive: a red-ribbon design on a yellow box printed with golden teddy bears and dolls in blue crinoline dresses, intertwined with Made in England 'Doll-in-Doll'. The dolls were only marked Made in England.

Fairy Teen
Doll Industries Ltd
20"/51cm
no markings
1959
Very similar to the Roddy dolls, this teenager has rooted short brown hair, sleeping eyes and five joints. She wears her original clothes – a white and silver lace and organdie dress with silver heeled sandals and a fairy wand. This doll still has her original box, marked 'Doll-in-Doll Made in England'.
(Collection Christine Wimsey. Photo by Phil)

DENYS FISHER
(Denys Fisher Toys of Lancashire)

Denys Fisher was an established children's toy manufacturer that came into the doll market with a few baby dolls in the early Seventies before manufacturing an 18"/45cm vinyl teen doll called Jaime in the late Seventies. The doll was made to represent a glamorous version of the Bionic Woman (Jaime Sommers) from the popular television series. This was a very pretty doll, with long, blonde rooted hair, attractive painted features, long slender limbs, well-moulded fingers, and arched feet that enabled her to wear high-heeled shoes. The doll was fully jointed but unmarked. Originally, she came dressed in a glamorous golden evening gown, with jewellery and white heeled shoes. Other outfits soon became available for her, all in a sophisticated style and modelled on the more glamorous outfits from the TV show.

Jaime
Denys Fisher Ltd
18''/45cm
none
1979
Jaime was the larger version of Jaime Sommers (Bionic Woman) and is depicted next to the reverse of her box showing her glamorous golden evening gown. The other side of the pink cellophane fronted box displays her name in white capitals. (Collection Christine Wimsey)

Jaime
Denys Fisher
18"/45cm
1979
*Jaime showing her glamorous hairstyle
and golden evening gown.*

Jaime
Denys Fisher
18"/45cm
no markings
1979   •
*Jaime pictured in one of her separately
available outfits – an emerald green three-piece
suit with silver lurex brooch detail and button
fastening.*

FAERIE GLEN (Hook & Franks of London)

A range of larger vinyl teenage dolls appeared in the Sixties, made by Faerie Glen, these named dolls included: Mimi, a 14"/35cm doll with rooted short hair; Gigi, a 15"/38cm doll with rooted short hair that came in her bra, panties and high heeled shoes; and Jackie, a 20"/51cm tall doll with rooted short hair who came dressed in a variety of beautifully made outfits – her evening gowns were of satin and velvety flock fabrics. These dolls had short, rooted blonde or brunette bubble-cut hair and painted lips and finger nails, and had five movable joints (head, arms and legs).

The company also produced a lovely range of beautifully made outfits and accessories for teenage dolls in five sizes at pocket-money prices. There was nightwear, daywear, sportswear, eveningwear, and accessories that included hats, coats and handbags. From 1960, many of these fashionable sets had names. For example: 'Adele' was a cotton organza frock; 'Carol' a frock and jacket; 'Betty' a jumper and trousers; 'Sandra' a nylon seersucker frock; 'Valerie' a cotton frock with belt; 'Gwen' a cotton frock with Beach Hat; 'Jill' a tartan skirt and blouse; and 'Margo' a glazed cotton frock and hat.

While the clothes were often marked individually with little 'Faerie Glen' tags, the dolls (presented in cellophane-fronted boxes) were unmarked and once out of the packaging are quite difficult to attribute.

Gigi
Faerie Glen/Hook & Franks Ltd
15"/38cm
no markings
mid Seventies.
An attractive doll with nylon rooted bouncy brunette hair with sleeping blue eyes. This doll is fully jointed and wears her underwear stockings and high-heeled sandals. These dolls were also available in blonde.

Jackie
Faerie Glen/Hook & Franks Ltd 20"/51cm
no markings
mid Seventies
A taller teenager with short blonde rooted curls, sleeping eyes and jointed limbs. She wears her original ballgown of white flock spot nylon with black velvet bodice, which has been turned up to show off her original stockings and heeled sandals. Notice that the dress is pictured on the box below.

As illustrated at right but in her box.
(Collection Christine Wimsey. Photo by Phil.)

NISBET (House of Nisbet of Somerset)

In 1982, Nisbet introduced a series of fifteen porcelain coloured vinyl dolls in the My Little Girl series, depicting a little girl at three important stages of her life: pre-teen (10"/26cm), early-teen (13"/33cm) and older-teen (16"/40cm). There were five sets of dolls for each of the three ages/sizes, entitled 'Parasols and Sunshine', 'Ballet', 'Parties and Romance', 'Wedding Days' and 'Winter Wonderland'. All the dolls had painted features and were available with blonde, fair, auburn, brown or dark brown rooted hair. They had five movable joints (head, arms, legs) and slim teenage-style bodies and were dressed as follows:

Parasols and Sunshine dolls had brown shoulder-length hair and were dressed in an Edwardian country garden style, with long, pastel cotton dresses and lace-trimmed parasols. The 10"/26cm doll was called 'Garden Party', the 13"/33cm doll was called 'Afternoon Tea' and the 16"/40cm doll was called 'Promenade'.

Wedding Days dolls had blonde, short hairstyles and were dressed as a bride and bridesmaids in creamy white satin, lace and ribbon-trimmed long dresses. The 10"/26cm doll was called 'Bonnie Bridesmaid', the 13"/33cm doll was called 'Maid in Waiting' and the 16"/40cm doll was called 'Bewitching Bride'.

Parties and Romance dolls had short, fair hair and were dressed in pastel satin, lace-trimmed long dresses with pearl necklaces. The 10"/26cm doll was called 'Birthday Party', the 13"/33cm doll was called 'First Dance' and the 16"/40cm doll was called 'Debutante's Ball'.

Ballet dolls had dark-brown shoulder length hair and were dressed in white net ballet dresses with velveteen cloaks and floral headdresses. The 10"/26cm doll was called 'Arabesque', the 13"/33cm doll was called 'Dress Rehearsal' and the 16"/40cm doll was called 'First Performance'.

Winter Wonderland dolls had auburn hair and were dressed for Christmas with red velvet dresses trimmed with white fur and fur bonnets and muffs. The 10"/26cm doll was called 'Snowflake', the 13"/33cm doll was called 'Holly' and the 16"/40cm doll was called 'Noelle'.

The dolls were presented in cellophane-fronted boxes with little wrist tags, but the dolls themselves were marked only with the Nisbet logo.

Left to Right
Debutantes Ball
Nisbet
16"
'Bewitching Bride'
Nisbet
16"

Left to Right
'Birthday Party'
Nisbet
10"
'First Performance'
Nisbet
16"

Yvonne
Palitoy/Bradgate
21"/53cm
no markings
1975
An extremely pretty doll with attractively
painted eyes and features, long pale blonde
centre parted rooted hair and long slender
jointed limbs with well moulded fingers and
arched feet. She originally came window boxed
with a Parisian scene, wearing a chic
maroon/lilac dress and jacket with smart
beret, tights and heeled shoes.
The box stated 'Top Paris Fashion Model'.

PALITOY (Palitoy Dolls & Toys of Leicester)

Palitoy joined the large teenage doll race in 1960 with Debbie, a 20"/51cm vinyl doll with a blonde or brunette rooted ponytail, who came dressed in bra, panties, stockings and heeled sandals with a nylon dress. The doll was unmarked and is now difficult to identify.

Palitoy also produced the 20"/51cm and 15"/38cm tall sleeping-eyed Belinda Series of dolls in the early Sixties. These dolls came with individual names and were beautifully dressed, had jointed limbs, and various styles and colours of short, wavy rooted hair, which could be combed and shampooed. The dolls had nylon stockings, blue eye make-up and sleeping blue eyes; many also had jewellery, but none had painted nails. The dolls were unmarked, but carried a swing ticket stating that they were awarded the Certificate of Health and Hygiene.

The 15"/38cm dolls from the Belinda Series were: Sylvie, who came in a linen-look sleeveless twist dress over a lace underskirt, undies (bra, panties, slip, stockings) and heeled sandals; Linda, who came in a three quarter length jacket over a winter dress with a furry hat, undies and sandals; Jenny, who wore a lace-trimmed taffeta ballgown with flowers in waist and hair, undies, shoes and jewellery; Nurse Carol, who came in a full nurse's uniform with black stockings and shoes, and had flexible arms carrying twin-jointed babies wrapped in white lace shawls.

The 20"/51cm dolls from the Belinda Series had paper nylon petticoats, bra, panties, nylon stockings and white heeled strappy sandals. Renee wore a flocked nylon net and taffeta evening dress; Annette had a blouse and polka-dot skirt and matching hat; Arlene came with a silver lurex bodice and black velvet swirl skirt; Deirdre had a spotted flocked nylon ballroom dress and jewellery; Luana was a coffee-coloured doll in a grass skirt with coloured bra and panties, flowers in her hair and a bead necklace; Janine – Scooter Girl came in a blouse, suedette jacket and checked skin-tight trousers; Janine – Ski Girl wore a windcheater jacket, blouse and skin-tight leopard print trousers; while Bride wore a white rayon brocade bridal gown with nylon net veil, underskirts, bouquet of roses and pearl necklace and earrings; and Ballroom Queen came in a long pastel satin ballgown, elaborately trimmed with ribbon and lace, petticoats, pearl necklace and earrings. These larger teenage dolls were superseded by the new 12"/30cm Tressy in 1964 (see page 181).

Sheena, an 18"/46cm model with a 'growing hair' feature was introduced in the early Seventies. Her long, fair hair could be shortened or lengthened by

Deirdre
Palitoy/Cascelloid Ltd
20"/51cm
Palitoy
Early Sixties
Brunette teenage doll in a spotted flock nylon dress in six layers making a full circle, nylon stockings, undies, heeled shoes and pearl earrings. The box is a fairly plain stripe.

Mary Make-Up
Palitoy/Cascelloid Ltd
20''/51cm
'Palitoy' on the back of her neck
1980
This doll came with make-up and hair-colouring sticks, as her name suggests. She had long rooted centre parted blonde hair, painted eyes and features. She is pictured in her original outfit with instruction leaflet and make-up. A further four outfits were available for her.

winding a key in her back which wound the hair up or down through a hole in the top of the head. She had an unusual 'character' face with blue sleeping eyes. Her original outfit was a pale mauve lurex two-piece trouser suit. Many more equally attractive outfits were available for this doll, including: 'Belle of the Ball', a pretty nylon ballgown; 'Summertime', a floral nylon dress; 'Cap-it-all', a dress jerkin and cap; and 'Anchors Aweigh', a striped top, skirt and jacket.

Mary Make-Up, introduced in 1980 was the re-launched 20"/51cm version of a doll first introduced as a 12"/30cm teen doll in the early Sixties. Nothing like her smaller sister, this larger teen doll had long centre - parted rooted pale blonde hair and delicately painted features, and was presented dressed in a long-sleeved pink floral dress and pastel-pink pinafore, with colour sticks for colouring the hair and a make-up set with brush and comb. The doll was presented in a cellophane-fronted box, had jointed limbs and flat feet with white flat-heeled pumps, but was unmarked and without a maker's logo. Additional outfits for Mary Make-Up included: trousers and smock top; skirt, blouse and matching waistcoat; pinafore dress with toning blouse; and a pretty party dress with a Cinderella-rags pointed hemline.

Palitoy Bradgate, the company's wholesale division, also launched a 20"/51cm teenage doll called Yvonne, 'Top Paris Fashion Model', who wore a chic maroon/lilac dress and jacket with matching beret. The doll was extremely pretty, with delicate painted features, long slender fingers and arched feet, pastel lips and rooted long, pale blonde centre-parted hair. Her window-fronted box was decorated with Parisian scenes, but the doll was unmarked.

The reverse of Sheena's box showing her long curled up growing-hair style and original outfit of lilac/mauve lurex trouser suit.

Sheena's 'Cap it All' outfit of cap, plaid dress and sleeveless coat in shocking-pink brushed cotton with white button trim. Shown in mint condition, still in pack.

Nurse Carol
Palitoy/Cascelloid Ltd
15"/38cm
Palitoy
Early Sixties
A brunette Nurse Carol in blue/white nurses uniform carrying twin jointed 3 $\frac{1}{2}$"/9cm babies wrapped in white lacy shawls. The doll was also available with blonde rooted hair. Nurse Carol's box was a plain brown carton.

Sheena
Palitoy/Cascelloid Ltd.
18"/45cm
Palitoy on the back of her head
1974
'Just like magic, her hair grows!' was the advertising slogan used for Sheena. She has a growing-hair mechanism with a winding key in her back which wound her the fair hair up or down through a hole in the top of her head. With sleeping blue eyes and an unusual character face she was an attractive five-jointed doll with very long contoured fingers.

Sheena
Palitoy/Cascelloid Ltd
18"/45cm
Palitoy on the back of her head
1974
Sheena pictured in her original lilac lock-knit nylon trouser suit.

PEDIGREE (Pedigree Dolls & Toys of Canterbury)

In the late Fifties, Pedigree introduced teenage dolls that were largely unmarked – most of their dolls from this period having only the Pedigree signature-style gold-tone brooch pinned to their clothes. The dolls had twist waists and movable arms, legs and head and came with nylon undies (bra, panties and petticoat), nylon stockings and high-heeled strappy sandals, usually in white; many came with pearl drop earrings as standard. Most dolls were individually named and beautifully attired, although a doll dressed only in her undies (for dressing at home) was also available in the 15/16" and 19/20" (38/40cm & 48/51cm) ranges. The hairstyles for these dolls were referred to as a Roman bob, bubble cut, bouffant (all short styles) and long ponytail. At first they had blue sleeping eyes, but in 1962 some were issued with brown sleeping eyes. The 19/20" (48/51cm) size had painted finger- and toe-nails.

In 1960, the 15/16" (38/40cm) teenage dolls were: Shirley, dressed in a black taffeta dress with stole; Marilyn, wearing a printed cotton dress; Zena, in a Swiss cotton afternoon dress; Merle, in a skirt and sweater; Vicki, in a velvet coat and dress; and Bride, in a white rayon mesh dress with taffeta petticoats, headdress and veil, and with a bouquet of Lily of the Valley flowers. By 1961, the dolls were updated and new ones added – Julia, Delia, Marilyn, Tanya, Myrtle and a new Bride. In 1962, the dolls were updated again and again given new names (Sylvia, Josephine, Rosalie, Kitty, Fleur, Rita, Kiki and Vida), and again in 1963 (Maureen, Coral, Genevieve, Gigi and another new Bride). Each time, some of the dress styles were repeated in different colours, while others had completely new designs; the Bride outfits were always updated.

There were so many named dolls, and all were so beautifully attired in late Fifties fashions, that it is a pity they were played with at all, as so many have consequently been destroyed. Today, there are only a few surviving examples of these lovely dolls in their original and mint condition.

Pedigree's 19/20" (48/51cm) teenage dolls, issued in 1960, were: Paula, dressed in a white and blue evening dress; Sandra, wearing a white and turquoise cotton day dress; Lorna, in a yellow blouse and turquoise cotton skirt; Marlene, with a black-and-white hat and coat over a red-and-white printed cotton dress; Yvonne, who wore a gold lurex thread cocktail dress and stole; Vanessa, in a blue and white flock sprayed nylon party dress; Monica, who sported a peacock blue-and-black print dress; Petula, dressed in a deep blue pleated skirt dress with white waffle cotton revers; Pearl, wearing a pretty floral sprig cotton dress and pearl earrings; and Bride, who wore a white taffeta short bridal gown, lace coatee with scalloped fronts, a headdress, veil, diamante earrings and a ring, and carried a lovely bouquet of flowers. In 1961 the outfits on these 19/20" (48/51cm) teenage dolls were changed only slightly in design and colour. By 1962, new 19/20" (48/51cm) dolls were introduced: Katrina, Eunice, Doris, Anthea and a new Bride. For 1963, the new names were Jacki, Laura, Cecile and another new Bride.

Pedigree's top of the range doll was the Miss Debutante series of 20"/51cm tall teenage dolls, introduced in 1960. All had movable waist, legs, arms and head and had the Roman bob, bubble cut or long ponytail hairstyles in one of several colours, from pale blonde, fair, auburn, brunette to black. They came dressed in underwear, nylon stockings and high-heeled shoes, and they had exquisitely detailed outfits in the finest fabrics. Their names and descriptions were: Theda, wearing a flocked terylene short strapless evening dress lined with taffeta, a waist slip, bra and panties, high-heeled evening shoes and pearl jewellery; Louretta, in a printed glazed cotton dress and matching hat, stole and handbag, a frilled waist slip, bra, panties, nylon stockings, high-heeled shoes and pearl earrings; Karen, who came in a crystal taffeta ballgown with train and white plush stole lined with the same taffeta as the dress, a petticoat, bra, panties, nylon stockings and high-heeled shoes; Vivienne, who sported a printed glazed cotton dress, with matching coat, hat and bag, with frilled undies, pearls earrings and shoes; a Bride, who wore a white satin and lace gown with headdress, veil, and undies trimmed in blue ribbon plus high-heeled shoes; and a Bridesmaid, who was presented in a taffeta and nylon organdie gown, headdress, bouquet, pearl earrings, undies and high-heeled shoes.

By 1961 the Miss Debutante series was updated with four new dolls: Antonia, in a pink-and-white sateen dress, with matching hat and bag; Michelle, wearing a short, blue-nylon evening dress and coat with evening shoes; Gala, who wore a deep lilac evening gown with matching sash and stole and headband; and Beverley, who wore a white crystal satin bridal gown, headdress, spotted veil, pearl necklace and earrings, and carried a rose bouquet. From 1962 two new dolls were added: Gay, in a colourful cotton print dress and hat, and Gypsy, with black hair and a red flamenco dress with black trim and high-heeled shoes. In 1963, the two new dolls were Clarissa and Cynthia, with updated clothes similar to the 1961 style of dresses.

As well as the larger teenage dolls, Pedigree introduced two smaller models in 1959/60: Miss Suzette and Little Miss Vogue, both of which had separately boxed outfits to collect.

Miss Suzette was $9\frac{1}{2}$"/24cm tall, was fully jointed, made of hard plastic and came with a rayon wig, a cami-knicker set, stockings and high-heeled shoes. Separately boxed outfits for her were: (A) afternoon dress in white cotton with red trim; (B) taffeta evening dress with spot trim; (C) white nylon evening gown with taffeta underskirt; (D) blue check cotton day dress; (E) printed red cotton summer dress; (F) beachwear of sunsuit, jacket and beach bag. This doll was only on the Pedigree Price List for a year and has never been seen by collectors, so one wonders whether it actually went into full production.

Little Miss Vogue, who was 10"/26cm tall, was a vinyl teenage doll with a twist waist, arched feet, rooted chrysanthemum-cut blonde, auburn or brunette hair, blue sleeping eyes, painted lips and finger nails. She came wearing a girdle and stockings, heeled sandals and pearl earrings. Her little booklet shows many fashion clothes that were available for these dolls – underwear, beachwear, day dresses, cocktail- and evening-dresses and bridal gowns in a range of lovely, shimmering cotton, nylon, and taffeta fabrics. The dresses were not named, just numbered one to five on each page of the booklet. Little Miss Vogue was unmarked and by 1960 was issued in a 'Carry-me-Case' (a plastic window fronted carry case that held a doll, coat hangers and three ensembles of fashion clothes for 'day-time', 'cocktails' and 'night-time'. A few more outfits were made for her through the early Sixties, and there was another updated 'Carry-me-Case', with doll transfers on the front. She was discontinued in 1963, with a final set of clothes that included a gay floral skirt and blouse, a white party dress and a red-and-white winter sports outfit with hat and pom-pom.

Miss Pedigree was introduced in 1979 as a collector's series of six dolls for the older girl. The doll had blue sleeping eyes, long, silky and flowing blonde or brunette rooted hair and was made of the palest pink vinyl, resembling porcelain. Measuring a little shy of 15"/38cm tall, the dolls had five movable joints – the prototypes also had a twist waist, but this feature did not go into production, presumably to cut costs. The dolls were elegantly dressed in long cocktail- or evening-dresses with feather boas. Quite an expensive range, the dolls came in window-fronted boxes, were very pretty, designed to be collected rather than played with, and were all unmarked.

Miss Debutante

Pedigree Dolls & Toys
20"/51cm
no markings
1960

This illustration of the Debutante dolls in the 1960 catalogue, showing day dresses, evening dresses and a beautiful bride in an assortment of fabrics and hair colours and styles.

Myrtle

Pedigree Dolls & Toys
16"/40cm
no markings
1961

Myrtle wears a lime green and orange printed cotton dress with lime green collar and pockets. She has ash blonde bubble-cut rooted hair and pearl earrings.
(Collection Denise Slade)

Coral
Pedigree Dolls & Toys
15"/38cm
no markings
1963
Coral wears a lilac/purple check cotton dress trimmed with purple ric-rac braid, undies. She has shoulder length black wavy hair and amber sleep eyes. (Collection Denise Slade)

Sandra
Pedigree Dolls & Toys
20"/51cm
no markings
1960
Sandra wears a red and white spot dress with white pique collar and pockets. Her honey blonde fringed hair is tied in a ponytail. She has undies, stockings and red heeled sandals.

Coded 20/D3
Pedigree Dolls & Toys Ltd
20"/51cm
no markings
1960
Teenage doll with brunette bubble-cut hairstyle, pearl earrings, cream taffeta brocade undies and slip lace trimmed with nylon and strappy, heeled sandals. She has rosy cheeks, red nail polish on her fingers and toes, and a twist waist. Her box depicts several of the hairstyles for these dolls: ponytail, long wavy, bubble cut etc.

Little Miss Vogue
Pedigree Dolls
10 ½"/27cm
no markings
1959
A blonde haired Little Miss Vogue with her original box and clothes.
(Collection Christine Wimsey. Photo by Phil.)

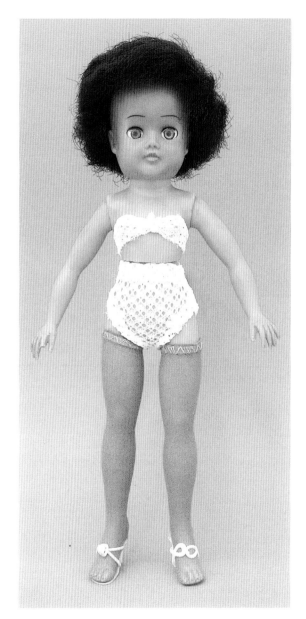

Little Miss Vogue
Pedigree Dolls
10 ½"/27cm
no markings
1959
Little Miss Vogue's hair was described in the little fashion booklet as a rooted chrysanthemum cut style and was available in blonde, auburn and brunette. She had sleeping blue eyes, six joints, including a twist waist, arched feet and pearl earrings. She is pictured wearing her undies and nylon stockings.

Little Miss Vogue
Pedigree Dolls
10 ½"/27cm
no markings
1959

On the left, a blonde wearing nylon gingham blouse with pink denim box pleated skirt. On the right a brunette wearing white crinkle cotton blouse and charcoal and white striped cotton skirt. From the range of daytime fashion outfits available for this doll.

Little Miss Vogue
Pedigree Dolls
10 ½"/27cm
no markings
1959

On the left a blonde wearing a red and white woven check taffeta day dress. On the right a brunette wearing a print beach outfit of swimsuit over skirt and towelling lined wrap. From the range of daytime fashion outfits available for this doll.

Little Miss Vogue
Pedigree Dolls
10 ½"/27cm
no markings
1959

Two silver and white dresses: on the blonde, a ballet dress trimmed with tinselled braid; on the brunette, a square necked bridal gown.

Little Miss Vogue
Pedigree Dolls
$10\frac{1}{2}$"/27cm
no markings
1959
*A cocktail dress with luminous stripes of gold, red
and silver for the blonde and a satin and lace
bridal gown for the brunette.*

*Two cellophane-fronted boxed outfits for Little Miss Vogue with original booklets:
(No. 26) blue and white flock printed nylon party dress with white lace trimmed
underskirt; (No. 34) turquoise/white fancy check printed cotton two-piece skirt and
blouse ensemble.*

Little Miss Vogue
Pedigree Dolls
$10\frac{1}{2}$"/27cm
no markings
1959
*A pale blonde Little Miss Vogue in her original blue
1960 Carry Case wearing a lemon/white gingham dress
with straw hat, heeled sandals and sunbrolly, plus extra
outfits of white jumper and red tartan skirt, lemon/blue
nightdress/negligee, stockings and shoes.*

Little Miss Vogue
Pedigree Dolls
10 ½"/27cm
no markings
1959

Two lovely evening gowns and coats: on the brunette, a sequin spotted
black net skirt over peach taffeta with matching duster coat; on the blonde,
a short evening dress of crepe and organdie with a white nylon fur coat.

Little Miss Vogue fashion booklet (1959)

Page from the Little Miss Vogue Fashion Booklet (1959),
showing sports wear, beach wear and separates, as well as an
assortment of afternoon, cocktail and evening dresses.

Little Miss Vogue
Pedigree Dolls
$10\frac{1}{2}$"/27cm
no markings
1959
A cocktail dress with luminous stripes of gold, red and silver for the blonde and a satin and lace bridal gown for the brunette.

Two cellophane-fronted boxed outfits for Little Miss Vogue with original booklets: (No. 26) blue and white flock printed nylon party dress with white lace trimmed underskirt; (No. 34) turquoise/white fancy check printed cotton two-piece skirt and blouse ensemble.

Little Miss Vogue
Pedigree Dolls
$10\frac{1}{2}$"/27cm
no markings
1959
A pale blonde Little Miss Vogue in her original blue 1960 Carry Case wearing a lemon/white gingham dress with straw hat, heeled sandals and sunbrolly, plus extra outfits of white jumper and red tartan skirt, lemon/blue nightdress/negligee, stockings and shoes.

Little Miss Vogue
Pedigree Dolls
10 ½"/27cm
no markings
1959
Two lovely evening gowns and coats: on the brunette, a sequin spotted black net skirt over peach taffeta with matching duster coat; on the blonde, a short evening dress of crepe and organdie with a white nylon fur coat.

Little Miss Vogue fashion booklet (1959)

Page from the Little Miss Vogue Fashion Booklet (1959), showing sports wear, beach wear and separates, as well as an assortment of afternoon, cocktail and evening dresses.

Clockwise from above

Miss Pedigree
Pedigree Dolls
15"/38cm
no markings
1979
This Miss Pedigree wears her original pink taffeta evening gown with feather boa and stands in front of her original black and golden trimmed box.
(Collection Christine Wimsey. Photo by Phil.)

Miss Pedigree
Pedigree Dolls
15"/38cm
no markings
1979
Miss Pedigree with an unusual outfit of brown striped and floral cotton long line top and frill at hem skirt, hat and toning light tan long boots. Her long blonde hair is braided into two plaits and pinned up under her hat.

Miss Pedigree
Pedigree Dolls
15"/38cm
no markings
1979
A pale, vinyl doll with the appearance of china. She has sparsely rooted long pale blonde centre parted hair, sleeping eyes, five joints and wears her original black halter-neck evening gown and feather boa.

RODDY (D.G. Todd & Co Ltd of Southport)

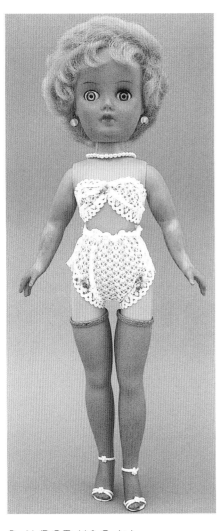

Roddy/D.G. Todd & Co Ltd
14"/35cm
'RODDY' on the back of the neck
1957
A lovely teenage doll with rooted short blonde curly hair, sleeping eyes, jewellery, undies, stockings and high-heeled sandals. She has six movable joints – head, arms, waist and legs.

This company began manufacturing teenage dolls in 1957, based on ideas about modern techniques of blow-moulding vinyl brought back from trips to the U.S.A. The dolls were approximately 14/15" (35/38cm) and 19/20" (48/51cm) in size and were usually marked 'Roddy' just below the hairline on the back of the neck. They came with a choice of bubble cut, feather cut and ponytail hairstyles in various shades of rooted saran, including platinum blonde, honey blonde, auburn, light brown and dark brown. They had blue sleeping eyes with lashes and painted lips, and some had painted fingernails and pearl earrings. Both dolls came with movable head, arms and legs and the larger doll also had a twist waist. They were supplied with realistic undies (bra, panties, petticoats, stockings) and white peep-toe shoes or white strappy sandals on arched feet. Several, with different hairstyles, were supplied in their undies only for dressing at home, while others came ready dressed and were boxed in a cardboard carton with pink diagonal stripes with the blue Roddy logo design over the front. Of the clothed dolls, the wonderful creative fashions they wore included a duster coat in cotton with matching hat and dress, a circular skirted rock'n'roll dance dress and matching bolero trimmed with white ric-rac braid with flouncy petticoats underneath, and evening gown of taffeta or chiffon with a matching stole, and bridalwear in white taffeta with glittering silver lurex thread, a headdress and veil with a floral bouquet and jewellery.

Named dolls were introduced in 1959 in the 19"/48cm size. Pamela had a bouffant hairstyle and wore a lurex patterned taffeta dress and hat with matching toning stole and a necklace. Claudine had a feather-cut hairstyle, earrings and black-and-white cotton duster coat and hat over a glazed cotton dress.

In 1961, five 14"/35cm dolls were introduced. Debbie had a bubble-cut hairstyle and wore a glittery nylon off-the-shoulder evening gown, nylon stole, pearl necklace and earrings and flowers in her hair. Bride wore a white nylon tulle over taffeta gown with glitter bodice and flounces, headdress and veil, pearl necklace and earrings and carried a bouquet. Cindy wore a candy-striped dress, Kym a floral striped dress and Peggy a striped and patterned cotton dress.

Many of these dolls had lovely fashionable clothes, made from glazed cottons, spotted and striped cottons, sparkly taffetas, chiffons, satins and nylons, but by the mid Sixties the company had been sold and production of the teenage dolls ceased.

Roddy/D.G. Todd & Co Ltd
Size: 20"/51cm
Marks: 'RODDY' on the back of the neck
Date 1959
A teenage doll with brunette rooted hair in a ponytail. She has sleeping eyes, five joints, arched feet and is wearing stockings. This is the tallest in the range.

Roddy/D.G. Todd & Co Ltd
16"/40cm
'RODDY' on the back of the neck
1957
A similar, but slightly taller, doll to the one on page 32. This one wears her undies and original red/white spot sundress with guipure daisy trim and stockings; she's missing her high-heeled sandals.

Roddy/D.G. Todd & Co Ltd
 20"/51cm
'RODDY' on the back of the neck
Date 1959
A lovely blonde, rooted, short curly-haired teenager with jewellery, original dress and stole, stockings and high-heeled sandals. She has sleeping eyes and stands next to her original box. This is the tallest of the Roddy teenage dolls.
(Collection Christine Wimsey. Photo by Phil)

33

ROSEBUD DOLLS & TOYS OF LEICESTER

Manufacture of Rosebud teenage dolls commenced in 1958 with two sizes: 15"/38cm and 20"/51cm tall. They had assorted hairstyles – bubble cut, long wavy and ponytail – in shades of white, blonde, auburn, brown, and pastel pink, blue, lilac and yellow. The dolls had sleeping eyes, realistic figures, jointed limbs, arched feet (with high-heeled sandals), straight waists, eye make-up, lip gloss and painted nails, and were usually marked 'Rosebud' within a key shape. The boxes were of pink-and-blue cardboard and were marked with the Rosebud logo within the key shape, across the centre lengthwise. These Rosebud dolls were not individually named, but the collections were.

The Fashion Right Fifteens 15"/38cm dolls were dressed in assorted cotton prints of spotted, striped, checked or floral shirt-waister style dresses, all with full skirts. There were also party dresses, dress-coat and hat ensembles, beach outfits that included a swimsuit, towelling jacket-hat and bag, glamorous chiffon, organza and nylon ball- and evening-gowns, jumper, trouser scarf and beret sets, and tartan dresses with white pique revers or collars. Some had hair of the same shade as their dresses. In addition, there was a Trousseau Box, which contained a teenage doll in a beach outfit with four extra outfits: a cotton hat and coat with spot trim; a glazed cotton day dress; a lace-edged pyjama set; and underwear and high-heeled shoes.

The Gay Twenties 20"/51cm teens were introduced between 1958 and 1961 and were similar to their 15"/38cm sisters with the same figure, hairstyles and colours. They were produced wearing nylon net ballgowns with silver ric-rac trim, flower- and lace-trimmed picture hats, undies and high-heeled sandals; floral cotton day dresses with matching sunhats, pearls, undies and sandals; floral cotton afternoon dresses with white pique revers and collars; checked gingham cocktail dresses with matching hats and toning accessories; brides in ballerina- and full-length white nylon and lace dresses with embroidered veils, rose bouquets, pearl earrings and necklaces, undies and sandals; french drill shorts and silky jersey sweaters; and shirt-waister blouses with full circular cotton print skirts.

The Rosebud Royal Range of 1961, also 20"/51cm tall, came in a special full-view perspex presentation box, to store the doll in and keep her dust free. These were marketed as "dolls with exclusive designer fashions for the more discerning customer". There were three dolls in this range:

(1) Wearing patterned satinised cotton hat and coat with black velvet trim, smart black handbag and shoes, pearl earrings and necklace, black lace-edged undies and nylon stockings.

(2) Continental shaggy fabric dresses with white plastic belts, brooch, beads and earrings, lace-edged taffeta undies, nylon stockings and shoes.
(3) Ballgown of slipper satin edged with lace and flowers, with swansdown stole and diamante pendant, earrings, tiara and ring. Stiffened petticoats, lace undies, nylon stockings and shoes.

The Royal Range dolls are not easy to identify once out of their boxes and devoid of their lovely clothes and accessories.

By the mid Sixties all of these teenage dolls had been phased out of the Rosebud range.

Miss Rosebud Teen
Rosebud Dolls Ltd
15"/38cm
Rosebud (1960s logo) Rosebud within a key shape across shoulders
1960
Miss Rosebud was re-launched in 1960 as a vinyl teenage doll in a wide range of outfits, from underwear to evening dresses. The dolls came in assorted hair shades – the one illustrated is white blonde – with sleeping blue eyes, blue eye makeup and red painted lips, finger and toe nails. This doll has lost her white, heeled sandals.
Miss Rosebud was also made in a series of 20"/51cm sizes

Miss Rosebud Teen
Rosebud Dolls Ltd
15"/38cm
Rosebud (1960s logo)
1961
She has a brunette long, wavy hairstyle and is wearing a nylon pleated skirt dress, undies, sandals and pearl earrings.

Gay Twenties Teen
Rosebud Dolls Ltd
20"/51cm
Rosebud (1960s logo)
1961
Blonde feather-cut, rooted hair, floral coat and hat over toning blue dress with lace-edged undies, nylons and sandals and pearl-drop earrings.

Miss Rosebud Teen
Rosebud Dolls Ltd
20"/51cm
no markings
1961
Doll with bouffant style brunette hair. Dressed in lilac floral satinised cotton skirt with matching lilac blouse, plus undies, stockings and sandals.

Miss Rosebud
Rosebud Dolls Ltd
20"/51cm
no markings
1959
Doll with brunette bouffant style hair, wearing red dress with large white circle design with white lapels and belt, undies, stockings and sandals.

Rosebud Dolls Ltd
no markings
14"/35.5cm
Rosebud (1960s logo)
early Sixties
A character face with rooted straight blonde hair tied in bunches, sleeping blue eyes, long painted lashes and finger nails. She wears jeans with a white self-patterned jumper, stockings and heeled sandals.

60s and 70s teenage dolls

This was the era of the smaller, 12"/30cm individually named dolls. Children knew their names through television advertising and as a consequence the dolls became household names. Dolls such as Sindy, Tressy, Daisy and Pippa were manufactured in their thousands each day to keep up with demand. They had beautiful wardrobes of clothes and accessories, and friends or 'family members'. In addition, dolls representing popular television programmes and films or popular singers or groups, were manufactured for the first time during this period.

These dolls are chronicled under their doll name rather than manufacturer's name.

"MATCHBOX"® ABBA

The world's most successful pop group, captured here in miniature for fans to own. Agnetta, Annafrid, Benny and Bjorn, all set to repeat their world wide musical success, this time across the toy counter.

Dolls
AB-101 Anna
AB-102 Frida
AB-103 Benny
AB-104 Bjorn

Dress Packs
AB-201 Japanese set
AB-202 Jump suit
AB-203 White and Gold set
AB-204 Money Money

AB-101 to **AB-104**
Available in 1 dozen solid packs. 0.015 cubic metres.
AB-200 Variety Pack of 12 dress packs.
3 each pack.
0.010 cubic metres.

AB-199/1 Starter Pack
4 each **AB-101** and 102
2 each **AB-103** and 104
1 each **AB-201** and 204
Plus headerboard and poster
0.018 cubic metres.

AB199/2
6 each **AB-101** and 102
1 each **AB-103** and 104
2 assorted dress packs plus headerboard and po[...]
0.018 cubic metres.

AB-203

AB-201

AB-202

AB-204

Agnetha (Anna), Bjorn, Benny,
Annifrid (Frida)
Matchbox/Lesney Products Co Ltd
Sizes: 8½''/21.5cm
no markings
1980
This illustration is from the 1980
Matchbox Catalogue and shows all four
ABBA dolls in their original white satin
outfits together with a few of the outfits that
were available in separate packs.

ABBA (Matchbox/Lesney Products Ltd, 1978)

In the late Seventies, Matchbox introduced four small dolls ($8\frac{1}{2}$"/21.5cm) representing the popular Swedish group ABBA. The dolls came fully dressed and there were additional clothing packs available that reflected many of the group's unusual and colourful stage costumes, many designed by the singers themselves.

Unsurprisingly, the dolls were named for the four singers: Anna (Agnetha), Frida (Annifrid) Benny and Bjorn. (The initials of their four names spelt ABBA, and made a palindrome that was easy to remember.) The dolls were vinyl and fully jointed with painted features. The boys had moulded fair hair, the girls came with long, rooted glossy hair – Anna's was blonde with no fringe and Frida's brown with a fringe. The dolls came boxed in cellophane-fronted purple boxes with all four singers on the front, pictured in concert. The boys were dressed in white satin trousers with coloured satin shirts, guitars and short white boots. The girls were dressed in short white shift dresses with an animal-print motif across the front; white knee-high boots finished the look.

The additional boxed outfits were entitled 'Japanese set', 'Jump Suit', 'White and Gold' and 'Money Money', the last also being the title of one of their hugely popular hit songs. The clothes were typical Seventies fashions of flared trousers with swinging fringed tops and long boots.

Produced towards the end of the group's career, the dolls were only in production for three years before ABBA, which consisted of two married couples, disbanded, divorced and each went their separate ways. The set of four dolls are not easy to find as they are unmarked and, without their clothes and boxes, difficult to identify.

Action Girl
Palitoy
$11\frac{1}{2}$"/29cm
'Uneeda Doll Co Inc MCMLXIX Dollikin ®
U.S. PAT 3010253 OTHER U.S. AND FOR
PAT PEND'
1971
Action Girl was boxed wearing a plain lock-
knit nylon jumpsuit in either dark pink,
lemon or turquoise with a floral sash (not
shown) and toning boots. She came with one
of three hair colours auburn (illustrated), fair
and brunette, painted features and fourteen
movable joints.

ACTION GIRL (Palitoy, 1971)

This doll was first introduced in the U.S.A. as Uneeda Dollikins in the late Fifties and introduced to Britain under licence by Palitoy as Action Girl in 1971. She had fourteen movable joints (head, arms, elbows, wrists, waist, legs, knees and ankles) and was a very versatile doll – a match for Action Man (see page 53) for little girls to play with. She was $11\frac{1}{2}$"/29cm tall and made of rigid vinyl, with a soft vinyl head, pretty face and neat features. Her eyes were painted bright blue and her lips pale pink. Her long waist-length rooted hair was straight and fringed and came in three colourways – fair, auburn and brunette. The doll could be posed in many lifelike positions, including kneeling and sitting in a chair. She was packaged in an attractive cellophane-fronted box dressed in a plain, lock-knit nylon jumpsuit with floral sash in lemon, turquoise or dark pink with toning short boots.

PINK CHAMPAGNE

CONTENTS:

A wonderful range of fashionable outfits was available separately for this doll. The clothes included trendy flared trousers, trouser suits, a poncho and maxi skirts – so reminiscent of the early Seventies – mini skirts, jerkins and legwarmers. The early 1972 named outfits included: 'Country Flare', a lemon trouser suit with matching bag and shoes; 'Wet Look', a black P.V.C. trouser suit with matching hat, scarf and shoes; 'Undercover Girl', a red maxi coat and hat with white scarf and shoes; 'Poncho Viva', a lemon jumpsuit and plaid poncho and shoes; 'Snake Charmer', a snakeskin hat and coat with tights and boots; 'Sports Girl', a P.V.C. jacket, blouse, trousers, scarf and shoes; 'Mini HaHa', a suedette coat, cravat, tights, boots and bag; 'Pop Festival', a lurex mini dress, tights, boots, handbag and necklace; 'Miss Capable', a cape, trousers, scarf and shoes; 'Snow Girl', a fun-fur coat and hat, boots and tights; 'First Night', a blouse with tie, waistcoat, trousers and shoes; 'Tank Top', a skirt, spot blouse, striped tank top; and 'Weekend Shopper', a blue-and-red coat with belt and bag.

In addition to the trendy outfits, many classic sets were available, too, including: 'Pony Club', jodhpurs, a jacket, scarf, hard hat, boots and crop; 'Alpine Holiday', ski pants, a Fair Isle jumper, hat and mittens, with skis and sticks; 'Ship Ahoy', white slacks, a striped top, navy jacket, cap and binoculars; 'Pick of the Pops', a floral jumpsuit with plain bodice; 'Boutique Beauty', trousers, a jumper and tank top; 'Star Performance', a mini skirt and jerkin; 'Theatre Time', a long floral skirt with white blouse; 'Getaway Girl', a two-piece trouser suit; 'Rambling Rose', a skirt and top with collar and tie decoration; 'Sunshine Set', a long-sleeved mini dress; 'Nurse', a dress, cap and apron, and cloak; and 'Ballerina', a calf-length chiffon dress with strap bodice, leotard and leg warmers.

43

Many more pocket fashions were available by 1973 in one- or two-item bubble packs, containing tops, skirts, trousers, belts, boots, bags, tights, skates, legwarmers etc. Also issued that year were 'Supersets' – 'Film Star', 'Beauty Queen' and 'Space Rover' – consisting of a luxuriously trimmed outfit with cardboard cut-out play scene and accessories.

On each box or pack were printed medallions, which the child could collect to replace with a real medallion necklace or a T-Shirt to wear.

As well as the Supersets, larger sets with more play value were introduced. They included: 'Pony Rider', which consisted of a model pony with nylon mane and tail, pony care accessories, and a sweater and jeans for Action Girl to wear; 'Four Poster Bed', a white, plastic four-poster bed with gold trim and white frilly canopy and coverlet in sparkly tricel; 'Wardrobe', a white plastic double-door wardrobe with golden trim and internal drawers and a set of coat hangers; and 'Chest of Drawers', again made in white plastic with two spacious drawers with safety mirror, trimmed in gold.

By 1974, Dancing Action Girl, with a similar face to the original doll and also $11\frac{1}{2}$"/29cm, had been introduced, boxed with her own dance record. By rotating her arm, she could be made to swivel and dance, turning at the waist and neck. This doll had ten joints, plus flexible, rather than jointed, knees; the ankles were now no longer jointed. She had blue painted eyes, pink lips and long rooted blonde, auburn or brunette fringed hair, and was presented wearing a pale pink dancing dress.

In 1974, the gift scheme was also updated and six printed medallions could now be exchanged for a medallion necklace, fourteen printed medallions for an outfit and twenty-one printed medallions for a friend called Jackie – basically the same as Dancing Action Girl, but dressed in a similar lock-knit nylon jumpsuit as the original Action Girl doll.

Action Girl was marked 'Uneeda Doll co Inc MCMLXIX Made in Hong Kong' on the back of the neck and 'Dollikin ® U.S. PAT 3010253 Other U.S. & for PAT PEND' across the shoulders. Dancing Action Girl was unmarked, as was friend Jackie.

Action Girl
Palitoy Ltd
11½"/29cm
'Uneeda Doll Co Inc MCMLXIX Dollikin ®
U.S. PAT 3010253 OTHER U.S. AND FOR PAT PEND'
1971
Three trendy fashions for Action Girl. Left to right: 'Snow Girl' fun fur coat and hat, boots and tights; 'Undercover Girl' red maxi coat and hat with white scarf and shoes; 'Poncho Viva' lemon jumpsuit and plaid poncho. The illustration also shows the three hair colours: brunette, fair and auburn.

Action Girl
Palitoy
11½"/29cm
'Uneeda Doll Co Inc MCMLXIX Dollikin ® U.S. PAT 3010253 OTHER U.S. AND FOR PAT PEND'
1971
A brunette Action Girl wearing 'Tank Top' skirt, spot blouse, striped tank top and white shoes.

Original Action Girl Fashion Magazine.

COUNTY FLARE

CONTENTS:

Trouser Suit · Bag
Shoes

Cat. No. 32810   Empire Made

WET LOOK

CONTENTS:

P.V.C. Trouser Suit
Hat · Scarf · Shoes

Cat. No. 32811   Empire Made

UNDERCOVER GIRL

CONTENTS:

Maxi Coat · Hat
Scarf · Shoes

Cat. No. 32812   Empire Made

PONCHO VIVA

CONTENTS:

Jump Suit · Poncho
Shoes

Cat. No. 32813   Empire Made

SNAKE CHARMER

CONTENTS:

Snakeskin Hat and
Coat · Tights · Boots

Cat. No. 32814   Empire Made

SPORTS GIRL

CONTENTS:

P.V.C. Jacket
Blouse · Trousers
Scarf · Shoes

Cat. No. 32815   Empire Made

SNOW GIRL

CONTENTS:

Fun Fur Coat · Hat
Boots · Tights

Cat. No. 32819   Empire Made

FIRST NIGHT

CONTENTS:

Blouse · Bell-bottom
Trousers · Bolero
Purse · Shoes

Cat. No. 32820   Empire Made

PINK CHAMPAGNE

CONTENTS:

Blouse with Tie
Waistcoat · Trousers
Shoes

Cat. No. 32821   Empire Made

*Fashions from the original Action Girl
Fashion Magazine show the wide
variety of outfits that were available.*

MINI HAHA

CONTENTS:

Suedette Coat
Cravat · Tights
Boots · Bag

Cat. No. 32816   Empire Made

POP FESTIVAL

CONTENTS:

Lurex Mini Dress
Tights · Boots
Handbag and
Necklace

Cat. No. 32817   Empire Made

MISS CAPABLE

CONTENTS:

Cape · Trousers
Scarf · Shoes

Cat. No. 32818   Empire Made

Action Girl
Palitoy
$11\frac{1}{2}$"/29cm
'Uneeda Doll Co Inc MCMLXIX Dollikin ® U.S. PAT 3010253 OTHER U.S. AND FOR PAT PEND'
Three classical outfits for Action Girl left to right: 'Tennis', 'Alpine Holiday' and 'Pony Club'. This illustration also shows fair, brunette and auburn haired dolls.

Two illustrations from Action Girl boxed items show the range of glamorous outfits available.

Clockwise from above:

Cellophane carded pack shows Action Girl's 'Ballerina' fashions.

A boxed fashion outfit showing 'Ship Ahoy'.

Two more cellophane carded packs showing the outfits 'Tank Top' and 'Weekend Shopper'.

Two cellophane carded packs showing Action Girl outfits. 'Nurse' consisted of a full nurse's uniform of blue dress with white collar and cuffs, black belt, royal blue cape with fob watch detail, white cap apron and shoes. A poster in the pack gives a simple guide to First Aid in words and pictures. 'Knightsbridge Set' comprises a pink and lime green cotton striped coat/dress with yellow leather-look collar and pockets, bag, shoes and chiffon scarf.

One of the Action Girl Supersets, 'Beauty Queen' included a cut-out play scene with clothes and accessories.

Superset 'Space Rover' included a cut-out play scene with clothes and accessories.

Superset 'Film Star' included a cut-out play scene with clothes and accessories.

49

Bedroom scene depicting Action Girl's 'Chest of Drawers' with mirror, 'Four Poster Bed' with drapes and 'Wardrobe' with double doors, drawers and hanging space.

The reverse of an Action Girl box showing the Action Girl furniture, the three colours of Action Girl's hair and the three coloured jumpsuits, plus the Medallion which the child could send for upon saving the required number of tokens.

Dancing Action Girl
Palitoy Ltd
11½"/29cm
no markings
1974
This doll had a similar jointed body to the earlier Action Girl, but the knees are flexible. She came only with pale blonde rooted long hair in a fringed style and was boxed with a record she could dance to – by rotating her arm she would swivel and dance to the music.

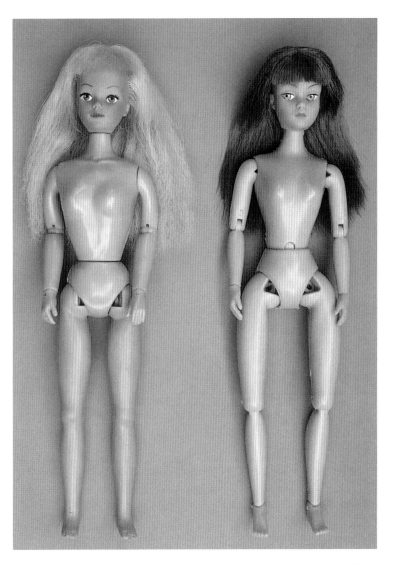

Naked Action Girl bodies, showing (on the left) the ten joints and flexible knees of Dancing Action Girl and (on the right) the fourteen joints of Action Girl.

Action Girl 'Pony Rider set, including: horse saddlery; sweater, jeans and boots; yard brush and bucket; grooming comb; grooming brush; backdrop; story book; and a Badminton Horse Trials map.
It is interesting to see that the sweater in the box was white, whereas it was pictured as blue on the box lid. The 'pony' is a brown horse from the same mould as Action Man's black horse.

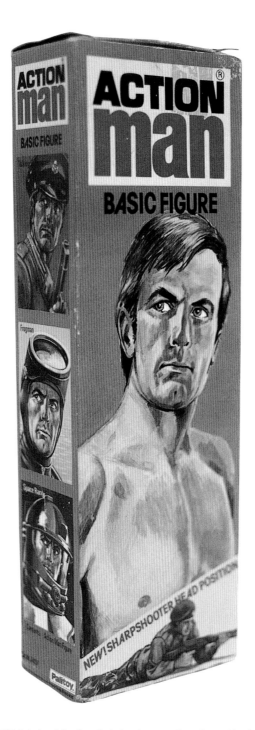

A 1980 Action Man box depicting the new 'Sharpshooter' head position, which consisted of a little indent in the neck plastic enabling the head to stay in a backward position while the figure 'fired' a rifle.

ACTION MAN (Palitoy, 1966)

Action Man was first introduced in 1964 as 'G.I. Joe', a 12"/30cm boy doll, by Hassenfeld Bros Inc in the United States. Never before had boys played with dolls; the closest thing was small model soldiers or perhaps a teddy bear, yet this new doll was for dressing and undressing just like the girl's playthings. Introducing boys to this new kind of male doll was something of a risk for a toy manufacturer, but G.I. Joe proved that Hassenfeld's research had been correct, as sales of this doll took off, surprising parents and manufacturers alike with the instant success and popularity it achieved. At first, the doll came with World War II Military Uniforms representing the U.S. Army, Airforce, Navy and Marines. His popularity peaked in the States with the start of the Vietnam War and many parents considered that the doll was now in bad taste and not the right influence for young children. Consequently, the 'Military Series' was discontinued in favour of the 'Adventure Series'.

By 1966, Hassenfield Bros and Hasbro Inc had been acquired by the giant General Mills Company, who also bought British Xylonite (as Mr A.E. Pallett's Cascelloid Company had been called since the late Thirties). Under the guidance of Hasbro Inc, G.I. Joe was introduced to Britain in that same year as 'Action Man', under the Palitoy trade name. As with G.I. Joe, the first Action Man dolls represented the forces – there was 'Action Soldier', 'Action Sailor' and 'Action Pilot', each with outfits and accessories, and, soon to follow, was 'Talking Action Commander', who could give eight different commands at random. Unlike G.I. Joe, however, Action Man remained popular for eighteen years, winning the National Association of Toy Retailers 'Toy of the Year' award on its launch in 1966. In 1973, and again in 1974, Action Man was awarded the 'Toys International Top Toy Trophy', and, in 1976, the 'National Association of Toy Retailers Ten Year Gold Award'. G.I. Joe's fortunes were not so good; in 1978 he was discontinued in the U.S.A., although he continued to be sold in many countries throughout the world.

The first Action Man, 12"/30cm tall like G.I. Joe, was a fully articulated plastic figure with twenty movable joints (head, neck, arms, biceps, elbows, wrists, double ball-jointed waist, legs, thighs, knees and ankles) that could be posed in many lifelike situations. He had moulded hair in three colours (brown, auburn and blonde), blue or brown painted eyes, and a handsome face modelled on twenty genuine U.S. heroes of World War II, with a scar on his right cheek. The Talking Action Commander model had a pull-cord voice mechanism and could give eight different commands at random.

Over the years, hundreds of authentically detailed uniforms and outfits were made for Action Man. There were the 'Military' uniforms of British Regiments, plus those of the U.S., Australian, Canadian, French, German and Russian armies in the 'Soldiers of the World' series; 'Famous British

Uniforms' depicted a British major, a military policeman, a grenadier guard and a Royal Marine, amongst others. An 'Adventure Series' included a policeman, a fireman, a frogman, an arctic explorer, an astronaut, a parachutist and a pilot. 'The Sportsmen' included a footballer, an Olympic champion, a karate expert and a cricketer, plus a go-kart and a sports car. 'The Wild West' included the 7th Cavalry as well as Cowboys & Indians; and 'Space Rangers' included captains, patrollers, aliens and a robot.

There was an element of history, ambition and fantasy with these dolls. Boys – and girls, with whom the toy was also popular – could learn about World War II, act out their ambitions to be firemen, policemen, explorers or sportsmen, or indulge in imaginary space adventures. Perhaps these are some of the reasons why the toy so enthralled children and remained popular for so long. Indeed, Action Man was only withdrawn from the market when the General Mills Group moved out of the toy industry in the early Eighties, with over thirty million dolls, uniforms and accessories sold. He was later remodelled and reintroduced in the Nineties.

Action Man was updated several times over the years, with flock-sprayed realistic hair introduced in 1970 along with bearded models, although the dolls were by then only available with dark brown or blonde hair in Britain. Gripping hands were added in 1973, but these early versions were quite fragile and little plastic covers were provided to protect the fingers while the men were dressed. Moving 'Eagle Eyes' (blue only) were introduced in 1976 and plastic joints replaced the metal pins; while the 'Sharp Shooter' head position and moulded-on blue pants arrived in 1979, and were the last of the body alterations. A 'Space Ranger' and 'Talking Space Commander' were also introduced in the late Seventies; these talking men now gave only five and six commands. New additions were 'S.A.S. Soldiers', 'Atomic Man', 'Tom Stone' (a black soldier), 'Bullet Man', 'The Intruder', 'Captain Zargon' with a 'Zargon Soldier' and 'Rom the Robot'. In all, over forty different body variations were made, as well as many vehicles, guns and accessories to collect.

The Action Man clothing was marked with a small, embroidered black-on-white label bearing the words 'Palitoy Action Man Made in Hong Kong'. The early clothing labels and boxes had six 'bullet holes' through the 'M' of Man, but after the mid Seventies this was deleted. The early boots were different, too, having stitch lines up the heel seam – later boots did not have this detail. In addition to clothing for the dolls, there was clothing for children – T-Shirts, sweatshirts, pyjamas, underwear etc – plus books, annuals, games, bedding, wallpaper, picture stickers, jigsaw puzzles, soaps and many other items, all bearing the Action Man logo.

Action Man Horse (mid Seventies).
For use with the Wild West or the Full Dress Horse Accoutrement set. Could also be used for Parades with Life Guards etc.

Both G.I. Joe and Action Man were made from rigid vinyl. Action Men dating from 1966 to 1978 are marked with 'Made in England by Palitoy under Licence from Hasbro © 1964' on their backs. Action Men from 1979, with plastic joints and moulded-on blue pants are marked '© CPG Products Corporation 1978', with 'Action Man' on the front of the moulded-on blue pants. The Eighties 'Sharp Shooter' head position is defined by a little indent in the neck plastic, enabling the head to stay in a backward position. On each Action Man box or pack, stars were printed for the child to cut out and collect to exchange for free gifts of clothing or accessories, or twenty one stars for a naked Action Man doll.

Action Man
Palitoy Ltd
12"/30cm
'Made in England by Palitoy Under Licence from Hasbro © 1964'
1966
The original Action Soldier, Action Sailor, Action Pilot and Action Commander, wearing their appropriate fatigues.

Four 1966 Action Man figures, with rigid vinyl bodies, moulded hair in three painted colours (blonde, auburn and brown), rigid hands and painted blue or brown eyes. The man on the right is a blonde Talking Action Commander who gives eight random commands when his cord is pulled.

The men are marked 'Made in England by Palitoy Under Licence from Hasbro © 1964' and have metal pin jointed limbs.

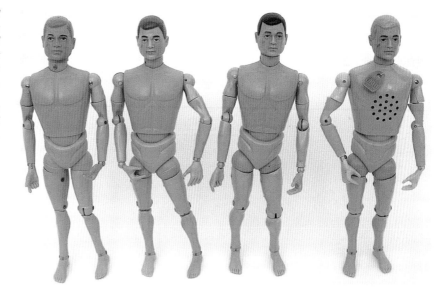

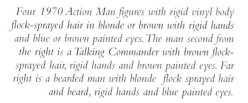

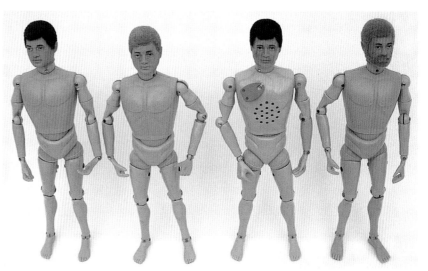

Action Pilot standing in front of his original box. Notice the bullet holes across the 'M' of Action Man – all early boxes and clothing labels had this detail.

Four 1970 Action Man figures with rigid vinyl body flock-sprayed hair in blonde or brown with rigid hands and blue or brown painted eyes. The man second from the right is a Talking Commander with brown flock-sprayed hair, rigid hands and brown painted eyes. Far right is a bearded man with blonde flock sprayed hair and beard, rigid hands and blue painted eyes.

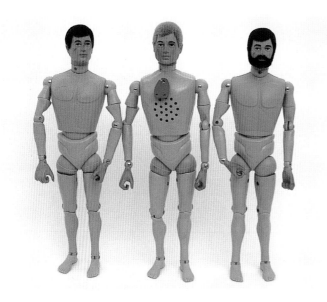

Three 1973 Action Man figures with rigid vinyl bodies, flock sprayed hair in blonde or brown. They have gripping hands which were quite fragile (little plastic covers were provided with them to protect the fingers for dressing). They have painted eyes in blue or brown. The man in the centre is a Talking Commander, with gripping hands, blonde flock-sprayed hair and blue painted eyes. On the right is a bearded man, also with gripping hands and brown flock-sprayed hair and beard.

The men are marked 'Made in England by Palitoy Under licence from Hasbro © 1964' and have metal pin jointed limbs.

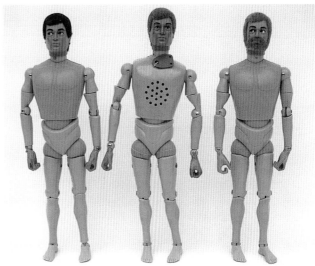

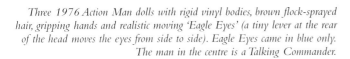

Three 1976 Action Man dolls with rigid vinyl bodies, brown flock-sprayed hair, gripping hands and realistic moving 'Eagle Eyes' (a tiny lever at the rear of the head moves the eyes from side to side). Eagle Eyes came in blue only. The man in the centre is a Talking Commander.

The men are marked 'Made in England by Palitoy Under Licence from Hasbro © 1964', and have metal pin jointed limbs.

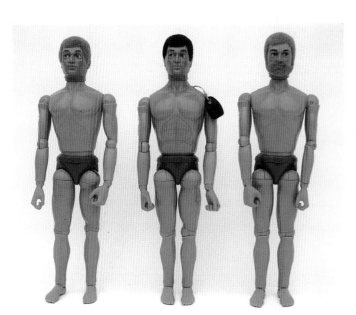

Three 1979 Action Man figures with rigid vinyl bodies in a dark bronzed flesh colour and moulded blue pants with 'Action Man' across the waistband. Each doll has plastic joints, firmer gripping hands, blonde or brown flock-sprayed hair and moving 'Eagle Eyes'. The man in the centre is Talking Commander.

The men are marked: © CPG Products Corporation 1978 and have plastic jointed limbs.

Action Man
Palitoy Ltd
12"/30cm
*'Made in England by Palitoy Under licence
from Hasbro © 1964'*
early Seventies
*British Soldiers: left to right: Tom Stone, the
Commando; a Royal Marine in full combat
uniform; a Parachutist in combat uniform; and
a Tank Commander. All have their original
'cloth' berets.*

Action Man
Palitoy Ltd
12"/30cm
*'Made in England by Palitoy under licence from
Hasbro © 1964'*
early Seventies
*Escape from Colditz: on the left a German
Camp Kommandant outfit; on the right a
British Escape Officer.*

Clockwise from top left:

Action Man
Palitoy Ltd
12"/30cm
'Made in England by Palitoy under licence from Hasbro © 1964'
early Seventies
Battle of Britain: on the left a Battle of Britain Pilot; on the right a German Luftwaffe Pilot.

Action Man
Palitoy Ltd
12"/30cm
'© CPG Products Corporation 1978' and 'Action Man' across the waistband'
late Seventies
Medic with Red Cross flag, stretcher, crutch and first aid kit.

Action Man
Palitoy Ltd
12"/30cm
'Made in England by Palitoy under licence from Hasbro © 1964'
mid Seventies
British Army Major with Special Operations Tent.

Action Man
Palitoy Ltd
12''/30cm
'Made in England by Palitoy under licence from Hasbro © 1964'
mid Seventies
RAF working dress with searchlight.

Action Man
Palitoy Ltd
12''/30cm
*'Made in England by Palitoy under licence
from Hasbro © 1964'*
1973
*Talking Commander with officer's cap, jersey,
trousers, boots, waist belt, pistol and holster.*

Clockwise from far left:

Action Man
Palitoy Ltd
12"/30cm
'© CPG Products Corporation 1978' and 'Action Man' across the waistband.
late Seventies
SAS Commando with bullet proof jacket, gas mask, and machine gun.

Action Man
Palitoy Ltd
12"/30cm
'Made in England by Palitoy under licence from Hasbro © 1964'
mid Seventies
Mountain and Arctic Uniform worn by patrols in sub zero temperatures.

Action Man
Palitoy Ltd
12"/30cm
'Made in England by Palitoy under licence from Hasbro © 1964'
Mid 70s, 105mm, Light gun with two royal marine soldiers in green cloth berets.

Action Man
Palitoy Ltd
12''/30cm
'© CPG Products Corporation 1978'
and 'Action Man' across the waistband.
late Seventies
*Scout Car with British Tank
Commander and British Soldier.*

Action Man
Palitoy Ltd
12''/30cm
'Made in England by Palitoy under licence from Hasbro © 1964'.
early Seventies
Left to right:
*Uniform: British Army Officer with Sam Browne Belt; Royal Air Force
Dress.*
*Uniforms: Sailor in square rig; Famous British Royal Military Police;
Soldiers of the World: British Infantryman; French Resistance Fighter;
Russian Infantryman; German Stormtrooper.*

Action Man
Palitoy Ltd
12''/30cm
'© CPG Products
Corporation 1978,
and 'Action Man' across
the waistband.
late Seventies
*American Jeep with
missile launcher and
American Paratrooper.*

Action Man (79)
Palitoy Ltd
12"/30cm
'Made in England by Palitoy under Licence from Hasbro © 1964'
early Seventies
Famous British Dress Uniforms, left to right: Grenadier Guard; Blues and Royals; Royal Hussar.

Action Man
Palitoy Ltd
12"/30cm
'Made in England by Palitoy under licence from Hasbro © 1964'
early Seventies
Famous British Dress Uniforms, left to right: 17th/21st Lancer; Argyll and Sutherland Highlander; Life Guard.

Action Man
Palitoy Ltd
12"/30cm
'Made in England by Palitoy under licence from Hasbro © 1964'
early Seventies
Sportsmen, left to right: Olympic Champion with gold medal; Judo expert with black belt; Footballer; Cricketer.

34810 Racing Car. Beautifully detailed push along racing car in kit form, with helmet, scarf and included.

34809 Go Kart. An authentically detailed Go Kart in easy to assemble kit form. Remote control unit gives finger tip steering, and forward and reverse control of the powerful electric motor (batteries not included). Complete with racing suit, scarf and helmet.

Action Man
Palitoy Ltd
12"/30cm
*'Made in England by
Palitoy under licence from
Hasbro © 1964'*
early Seventies
*Adventurer with beard
wearing jeans and sweater.
The earlier outfit had a
cream sweater and blue jeans.*

*Top: Page from the Action Man Manual depicting the Racing Car (1970)
in green with a yellow stripe and black number 7.*

*Above: Page from the Action Man Manual depicting the Go Kart.
This vehicle is self assembly.*

Action Man: Adventure Series
Palitoy Ltd
12"/30cm
*'Made in England by Palitoy under
licence from Hasbro © 1964'*
early Seventies
*Two Polar Explorers with husky dogs
and a sledge.*

Action Man: Adventure Series
Palitoy Ltd
12"/30cm
'Made in England by Palitoy under licence from Hasbro © 1964'
mid Seventies
Fireman on the left and Police Motorcyclist on the right.

Action Man: Adventure Series
Palitoy Ltd
12"/30cm
'Made in England by Palitoy under licence from Hasbro © 1964'
early Seventies
U.S. Mercury Space Capsule and two Astronauts.

Action Man: Adventure Series
Palitoy Ltd
12"/30cm
'Made in England by Palitoy under licence from Hasbro © 1964'
early Seventies
Mountaineer with clothing and equipment to carry out Mountain Rescue operations.

Action Man: Adventure Series
Palitoy Ltd
12"/30cm
'Made in England by Palitoy under licence from Hasbro © 1964'
early Seventies
Sea Wolf transport and Frogmen.

Action Man: Wild West
Palitoy Ltd
12"/30cm
'Made in England by Palitoy under licence from Hasbro © 1964'
mid Seventies
Left to right: 7th Cavalry; Cowboy Scout; Indian Chief.

Angels
Denys Fisher Ltd
$9\frac{1}{2}$"/24cm
no markings
1976
Angels Trainee Nurse standing in front of two outfit packs.
Private Nurse on the left and Staff Nurse on the right.

Angels
Denys Fisher Ltd
$9\frac{1}{2}$"/24cm
no markings
1976
Angels Trainee Nurse standing in front of two outfit packs:
District Nurse on the left and Sister on the right.

ANGELS (Denys Fisher, 1976)

Nurses have always been popular as play dolls, and this one's popularity was assured through its association with the BBC television programme Angels and was described as 'your favourite nurse from St Angela's hospital', the hospital depicted in that TV drama. The doll was unmarked, $9\frac{1}{2}$" /24cm tall, had rooted, centre-parted straight dark-brown hair tied back in a bun, painted blue eyes with a rigid vinyl body and six movable joints (head, arms, legs and waist). She came dressed as a 'Trainee Nurse', wearing an outfit that was available separately packed as well. There were four more separately packed outfits for her, too, entitled 'Staff Nurse', 'District Nurse', 'Private Nurse' and 'Sister'. 'Trainee Nurse' consisted of a striped dress, crisp white apron, nurse's belt and neat white cap with trainee stripes and black shoes. The 'District Nurse' outfit had a navy short-sleeved dress piped in white, navy belt, and hat with a shoulder bag and shoes. 'Private Nurse' was a short-sleeved white dress and cap with shoes. 'Sister's Uniform' was a navy-blue dress with white collar and special frilly cap with shoes. All the outfit packs came with a nurse fob-watch and badge and looked very realistic. A 'Hospital Ward' pack with a patient was also produced for added play value. This item was packed flat but could easily be self assembled. Several plastic accessories were supplied with it, including a bed (with the patient), trolley table, water jug, cups, plates, temperature chart and curtains to pull across for privacy. The doll is not easy to find and attribute once out of its packaging and clothing.

Angels
Denys Fisher Ltd
$9\frac{1}{2}$"/24cm
no markings
1976
This Angels Trainee Nurse was an attractive but petite delicate and tiny doll compared with other teen dolls.

Illustration from rear of box showing all five outfits available for the Angels nurse from St Angela's Hospital.

The Six Million Dollar Man
Denys Fisher Ltd
13"/33cm
'© 1976 Gen Mills Fun Group Inc By its Division
Kenner Parker Cincinnati Ohio 45202 Cat No
65000' across the shoulders.
*Taken from the catalogue, this illustration shows the
Six Million Dollar Man with his 'engine' and
wearing his red NASA suit and track shoes.*

DENYS FISHER 'SIX MILLION DOL-
LAR MAN' a 13 in. articulated action
figure in plastic, based on the popular TV
hero. Features ratchet-operated 'bionic'
arm which really lifts the dummy engine
supplied; 'bionic' eye, a viewing lens
which you can really see through; and roll
back 'skin' on his arm to reveal modules
which can be removed for 'bionic' surgery.
Dressed in N.A.S.A. suit and track shoes.

THE BIONIC WOMAN AND
THE SIX MILLION DOLLAR MAN
(Denys Fisher, 1976)

These two dolls were based on characters originally seen on television in 1974. U.S. Colonel Steve Austin (played by actor Lee Majors) was the Six Million Dollar Man, rebuilt after an accident that had left him virtually dead, to become better, stronger, faster than ever before – his spare-part surgery cost six million dollars, hence his name. Jaime Sommers (played by actress Lindsey Wagner) was the Bionic Woman, star of a spin-off series.

The Bionic Woman was 12 ½"/31cm tall with rooted shoulder-length blonde hair, painted eyes and features, and was marked 'General Mills Fun Group Inc 1976'. As one turned her head from side to side her ears would 'ping', just like her character on TV. Her right arm had bionic modules that were visible when the life-like vinyl 'skin' was rolled back. Her legs, too, had bionic modules with lift-up flaps over them. She carried a mission purse containing a comb, brush, mirror and cosmetics, as well as a wallet with bionic money, maps, codes and plastic cases – everything a girl could need for secret assignments or assignations with Steve Austin!

Roll back the life-like skin on her right arm to reveal Bionic Modules.

There are also Bionic Modules each leg, just lift up the flap to reveal them.

Jaime's NEW Mission Purse contains all this Comb, brush, mirror, pretend cosmetics and cosmetics case. Wallet with 'Bionic Money'.

Dressed in a royal-blue jumpsuit and red sandals, the Bionic Woman could hurtle off on her fabulous 'Superbike' from a turbo powered 'Tower of Power'. The complete set comprised a Bionic Woman figure in a special bike suit and helmet with the Superbike, launch ramp and power pump.

By day, Jaime was a schoolteacher. 'Jaime's School House and Communications Centre' comprised a flat-pack board partition schoolroom with desk, bookcase, files and books that were not what they seemed: the desk contained a secret panel and special video and buzzer system, the bookcase turned to reveal a secret communication centre, and the files and books were hollow to carry secret messages. On one partition there was a blackboard that the child could write on. The set also contained a school dress for Jaime to wear.

The Bionic Woman 'Designer Collection' of outfits were designed exclusively for Jaime and included four trouser suits for assignments and four long evening dresses for formal occasions. The named outfits were: 'Blue Mist', a blue two-piece trouser suit; 'Casual Day', a three-piece dark-blue suit; 'Silk 'n Satin', a white trouser-suit and top; 'Floral Delight', a frilly floral dress; 'Peach Dream', a sleeveless evening gown with wide sleeves; and 'Country Comfort', a long-sleeved red dress and over pinny.

A large movable styling head – complete with a tray of hairdressing accessories – was also advertised in 1976, depicting the face of Lindsey Wagner. The styling-head's hair could be set and styled.

The Six Million Dollar Man measured 13"/33cm and had moulded, painted brown hair, painted features and one bionic glass eye with viewing lens. He had a ratchet-operated bionic arm, which could lift his dummy engine, and two bionic legs, which were supposedly better, stronger and faster than those of any other man. Like the Bionic Woman, he, too, had modules on his arm under roll-back vinyl 'skin'. He was dressed in a red NASA suit and track shoes. Other outfits were available for him, including a 'Space Suit'. In addition, there was a 'Bionic Transport Repair Station', a cylindrical unit that could be opened to reveal a compartment into which the Bionic Man could be placed and connected to various 'cables' and 'read-outs' to effect 'repairs' to his bionic parts and 'recharge' his bionic system. He was marked '© 1976 Gen Mills Fun Group Inc By its Division Kenner Prod Cincinnati Ohio 452020 Cat No 65000' across the shoulders.

Facing page, clockwise from top left:

Bionic Woman
Denys Fisher Ltd
12½"/31cm
'General Mills Fun Group Inc 1976'
1976
The Bionic Woman dressed in a royal-blue jumpsuit with red sandals and mission purse standing next to her original box.

The rear of the Bionic Woman's packaging, showing all the Designer Collection outfits available for Jaime Sommers (the Bionic Woman).

The rear of the Bionic Woman's box, depicting her bionic modules, school house, fashion outfits and Styling Boutique.

A Designer Collection outfit, called Floral Delight, for Jaime Sommers (the Bionic Woman).

The Six Million Dollar Man
Denys Fisher Ltd
13"/33cm
'© 1976 Gen Mills Fun Group Inc by its Division Kenner Prod. Cincinnati Ohio 45202 Cat No 65000' across the shoulders.
On the right, the Six Million Dollar Man showing the roll-back skin on his right arm. On the left, shown in his Space Suit.

NEW
MISSION
PURSE

Jaime Sommers'
THE
BIONIC
WOMAN
BY DENYS FISHER

DESIGNER COLLECTION
FASHIONS FOR JAIME SOMMERS

THE BIONIC WOMAN

ALL OUTFITS SOLD
SEPARATELY ·
BIONIC WOMAN
DOLL NOT INCLUDED

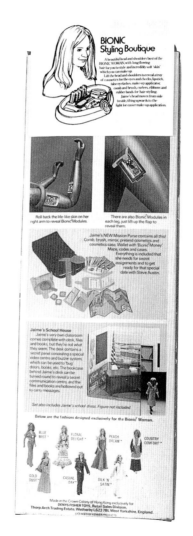

BIONIC
Styling Boutique

THE BIONIC WOMAN®

DESIGNER COLLECTION
FASHIONS FOR JAIME SOMMERS

CONTENTS: ONE FLORAL PARTY DRESS WITH MATCHING
SHAWL AND ORANGE PLATFORM SHOES

Blythe
Palitoy Ltd
11½"/29cm
'Blythe Kenner Products
Cincinnati Ohio 1972 General
Mills Fun Group Inc Pats
Pending' across shoulders
1972
A blonde Blythe standing in front
of her box. This doll has blue eyes
and wears 'Pretty Paisley' blue
and tan paisley patterned dress.
(Collection Christine Wimsey.
Photo by Phil)

BLYTHE (Palitoy, 1972)

Described as the 'fascinating doll with the surprise in her eyes', Blythe measured 11½"/29cm tall and, by pulling a cord in her back, her eyes would change from 'Bouncy Brown' to 'Beautiful Blue', 'Pretty Pink' and 'Green eyed and Groovy'. With each eye colour, one could change her expression and personality. The brown and pink eyes were forward facing and the blue and green eyes were side glancing. She came with one of four hair colours (blonde, auburn, brown and black) in a long straight style, with four additional curly wigs and matching sunglasses available in the same four hair colours. The wigs came on a wig stand with a brush and comb to style them. Because of the eye-change mechanism, the doll's head was unusually large, measuring 4½"/11cm, with two screws in her back securing the mechanism. Proportionally, the body was small at just 7"/18cm; it had a twist waist, jointed arms and legs and flexible knees.

A wide assortment of striking outfits were available for Blythe, with names such as 'Pretty Paisley', 'Roaring Red', 'Pow Wow Poncho', 'Medieval Mood', 'Pinafore Purple', Kozy Kape, 'Love'n'Lace', 'Pleasant Peasant', 'Aztec Arrival', 'Golden Goddess', 'Lounging Lovely' and 'Priceless Parfait'. In fact, all the clothes were brilliantly coloured typically Seventies Flower-Power and Aztec patterned outfits that matched her beautiful eyes. The doll was marked 'Blythe Kenner Products Cincinnati Ohio 1972 General Mills Fun Group Inc Pats Pending' across the shoulders. The doll was revamped and reintroduced in the 1990s under the name of Designer Girls.

Reverse of pack shows the Blythe doll with various hair and eye colours and states: 'Quick as a wink…Pull the ring in my back and my eyes change colour!' It depicts the carded sets of fashions (Pretty Paisley, Golden Goddess, Medieval Wood, Love-n-Lace, Roaring Red, Pinafore Purple, Pleasant Peasant and Lounging Lovely); the boxed sets of fashions (Priceless Parfait, Aztec Arrival, Kosy Kape and Pow Wow Poncho); and the new Blythe Wigs (Lemon, Lime, Strawberry and Blueberry). Each wig came packed with a pair of sunglasses and comb and brush set.

73

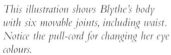

This illustration shows Blythe's body with six movable joints, including waist. Notice the pull-cord for changing her eye colours.

Blythe
Palitoy Ltd
11½"/29cm
'Blythe Kenner Products Cincinnati Ohio 1972 General Mills Fun Group Inc Pats Pending'
1972
A black haired Blythe wearing a dress that tones with all her eye colours – brown, blue, pink and green.

Blythe
Palitoy Ltd
11½"/29cm
'Blythe Kenner Products Cincinnati Ohio 1972 General Mills Fun Group Inc Pats Pending'
1972
The fascinating doll with the surprise in her eyes , Blythe is shown here with amber eyes – described in the catalogue as 'Bouncy Brown'.

Blythe
Palitoy Ltd
11½"/29cm
'Blythe Kenner Products Cincinnati Ohio 1972
General Mills Fun Group Inc Pats Pending'
1972
'Green Eyes and Groovy' Blythe with side-
glancing eyes dressed in green satin.

Blythe
Palitoy Ltd
11½"/29cm
'Blythe Kenner Products Cincinnati Ohio 1972
General Mills Fun Group Inc Pats Pending'
1972
'Pretty Pink' eyed Blythe, dressed in shorts and
gingham top.

Blythe
Palitoy Ltd
11½"/29cm
'Blythe Kenner Products Cincinnati Ohio 1972
General Mills Fun Group Inc Pats Pending'
1972
Blythe with 'Beautiful Blue' side-glancing eyes,
denim jeans and blue striped blouse.

Anna of the Champions
Pedigree
10$\frac{1}{2}$"/27cm
'0036001X' on the back of the neck
1977
*Two original Anna dolls – brunette and blonde,
wearing their original outfits. They are pictured with
their horse, Happytime, and one of the fences, Posts
and Rails, that were available for them.*

CHAMPIONS (Pedigree, 1975)

These fully articulated dolls with riding outfits and fully poseable horses were introduced by Pedigree in 1975. Anna with a Chestnut Pony called 'Happytime' and Peter with a Palomino Pony called 'Sundancer' were extremely popular for a few years. Boxed starter sets came with a special booklet written by Ann Moore – European Ladies Champion – relating real-life training and pony care tips for the child to follow.

Anna was $10\frac{1}{2}$"/27cm tall, with shoulder length blonde or brunette rooted hair in a curled up ends style that fitted under her hard hat, painted features and fifteen movable joints with a rigid vinyl body. She was first introduced dressed in beige riding breeches, yellow shirt, white/red spotted scarf and black hard hat and boots with a crop, and the back of her neck was marked '036001X'. She was updated a couple of years later and issued wearing riding breeches, red jumper, black hard hat, boots and crop. This newer model had a different, slimmer face and a short and neat hairstyle in blonde or brunette, trimmed to the ears; the body remained the same, but the back of the neck was marked '036153'. Many riding outfits were introduced for Anna, including separate show-jumping jackets and named outfits such as 'Jockey', 'Pony Club', 'Schooling', 'Trecking' and 'Point to Point'.

Peter came dressed in beige breeches, royal-blue jumper, black hard hat, boots and crop and had short brown rooted hair. He, too, was fully jointed, had painted features and was $11\frac{1}{2}$"/29cm tall. He was marked '040001' on the back of his neck. Peter had his own outfits but he could also wear the unisex riding outfits made for Anna.

Both dolls had 'Action Horses', with rooted manes and tails, for feeding, grooming and riding. As well as boxed fences, which were available separately and included 'Post and Rail', 'Cavalette' and 'Water Jump', there was a 'Stable', too, for all-round play value.

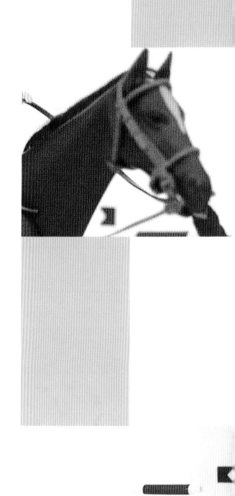

Peter of the Champions
Pedigree
11½"/29cm
'040001' on the back of the neck.
1977
Peter in his original outfit, with horse Sundancer and one of the jumps available.

Anna of the Champions
Pedigree
10½"/27cm
'036163' on the back of the neck.
1980
Two later 'Schooling' Anna dolls, wearing dungarees with a plastic embossed 'A' on their bibs. Pictured with the Happytime horse.

Right:
Anna of the Champions
Pedigree
$10\frac{1}{2}$"/27cm
'036153' on the back of the neck.
1979
Two later Anna dolls in their original outfits: a blonde and brunette with the Happytime horse and fence, available as extra toys.

Below:
Anna and Peter of the Champions
Pedigree
Sizes: $10\frac{1}{2}$"/27cm and $11\frac{1}{2}$"/29cm
'036001X', '044001' and '036153'
Dates: 1977, 1977 and 1979
Peter in the centre, with early Anna on the left and later Anna on the right.

8

This illustration shows two boxed outfits for Anna from 1975 to 1977: 22302 'Pony Club' and 22307 'Trekking'.

This illustration shows two boxed outfits for Anna from 1975 to 1977: 22305 'Point to Point' and 22306 'Show Jumping'.

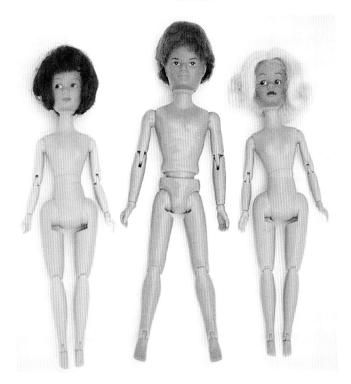

Anna and Peter of the Champions
Pedigree
Sizes 10½"/27cm and 11½"/29cm
'036153', '04001' and '036001X' l. to r.
1979 Anna marked 036153.
1977 Peter marked 04001.
1977 Anna marked 036001X.
All three marked on the back of neck.
Dates: 1979, 1977 and 1977
This illustration shows the fourteen movable joints on these dolls. On the left early Anna, on the right later Anna. All the dolls had painted features and rooted hair. Both Anna dolls were available with blonde or brunette hair, but Peter was only available with brown hair.

PEDIGREE 'CHAMPIONS'
FIGURES, OUTFITS AND JUMPS FROM 1975 to 1977

22300	Anna figure
22301	Happytime Horse for Anna
22302	Ponyclub outfit for Anna
22303	Schooling outfit for Anna
22304	Sidesaddle outfit for Anna
22305	Point to Point outfit for Anna
22306	Showjumping outfit for Anna
22307	Trekking outfit for Anna
22308	Not issued
22309	Cavalette jumps
22310	Post and Rail jumps
22311	Champion Showjumpers pack
22312	Not issued
22313	Peter figure
22314	Showjumping outfit for Peter
22315	Ponyclub outfit for Peter
22316	Jockey outfit for Peter
22317	Water Jump pack
22318	Not issued
22319	Stable
22320	Sundancer Horse for Peter

Charlie's Angels
Palitoy Ltd
8 ½"/21.5cm
'Spelling Goldberg Productions 1977' marked across lower back
This illustration shows 'Sabrina' on the left, 'Jill' next to her, 'Kelly' in her cellophane-fronted pack and little sister 'Chris' on the right. The writing on the pack states: 'Ages 4 to 12. Doll Jumpsuit Scarf & Boots. Fully jointed 8 ½" doll with twist'n'turn waist and rooted nylon hair that you can style'. The reverse of the pack was blank.

CHARLIE'S ANGELS (Palitoy, 1977)

These dolls originated from an extremely popular American television series that crossed the Atlantic in the mid Seventies. The dolls were made under licence to Spelling Goldberg Productions in 1977 (as marked on their lower back) and were marketed by Palitoy.

There were three dolls at first, based on the three female characters in the TV programme. Sabrina (as played by actress Kate Jackson, who, it is said, was the person who first suggested the idea of a "Girl Cop Series" to the Spelling Goldberg Production Company); Jill (Farrah Fawcett Majors); and Kelly (Jaclyn Smith). The pretext of the story was that there were three beautiful girls working for a private eye called Charlie (John Forsythe, who was never seen, you just heard his voice over the telephone), who were hired to solve dangerous murders, smuggling and kidnap cases – hence "Charlie's Angels". When Farrah Fawcett Majors left the series she was replaced by a younger sister, Chris (played by Cheryl Ladd), who was later issued as a doll. In the TV series, Sabrina was replaced for one season by a new character played by Shelly Hack and then another played by Tanya Roberts for a short while until the series came off air. These last two characters were not issued as dolls in Britain.

The four Charlie's Angels dolls that were produced were 8 $\frac{1}{2}$" /22cm tall, fully jointed and, although small, bore an uncanny resemblance to the actresses they were based upon. Sabrina had dark brown shoulder length straight hair; Jill had a honey blonde flick up style; Kelly had chestnut shoulder lengthy wavy style; and little sister Chris had a long blonde style. The dolls' clothing echoed the glamorous and glitzy Seventies styles worn
in the TV series: jumpsuits, trouser suits, long sparkly nylon dresses, skirts and trousers, and long chiffon evening dresses.

These petite doll heads had no marks. Once out of the carded packaging and attractive clothing, they are difficult to identify or attribute.

Daisy's own Bike, pictured with a Standard Daisy and the original box. The cycle pedals actually turned the wheels enabling Daisy to 'ride' it.

DAISY (Model Toys, 1972)

British company, Berwick Timpo Ltd formed Flair Toys to sell and distribute the 9"/23cm fashion teenage doll Daisy, manufactured by Model Toys in Hong Kong. She was designed by Mary Quant and named after the 'daisy' trademark that appeared on all Mary Quant-designed products. Daisy was a pretty, vinyl doll with curly, shoulder-length honey-blonde rooted hair, painted left-glancing blue eyes, turquoise eyeshadow and an extensive range of Sixties and Seventies outfits, designed by Mary Quant herself.

Several versions of Daisy were made during the early Seventies, including: 'Darling Daisy', the standard model, with honey-blonde hair, jointed head, arms and legs, flexible knees and a twisting waist; 'Brunette Daisy', the same as Darling Daisy but with chestnut curly rooted hair; 'Skating Daisy', who had streaked blonde hair but was otherwise the same as Darling Daisy; 'Dizzy Daisy', a budget version of the doll with honey-blonde rooted hair, a straight waist and straight non-bending legs; and 'Dashing Daisy', the deluxe version of the doll, with a swivel-jointed hips, flexible arms, and a twisting head and waist (Dashing Daisy also had her own horse called 'Archie').

Daisy's friend, Amy was available free by collecting twenty-two white 'Daisy tokens', cut from the Daisy boxes and redeemed by posting them to Flair Toys. Amy resembled Budget Daisy with the straight legs, but had rooted dark-brown hair in a short side-parting style.

By the late Seventies, several more Daisy dolls had been introduced, including: 'Three Style Daisy' with right-glancing painted eyes, who came boxed with three different styles of wigs for her to wear – a short brunette style, a shoulder-length blonde straight-fringed style and an auburn curly style; 'Walking Along Daisy', boxed with a Dalmation Dog called 'Spot'; and 'Country Style Daisy', sat in her own swing, hung from a plastic tree branch. All of these dolls were the same size as Darling Daisy. To commemorate the Queen's Silver Jubilee in 1977, a 'Britannia Daisy' was introduced for just one year, dressed in a Union Jack printed dress and packaged in a 'London Scenes' printed box.

'Daisy Long Legs', which had a similar face to the other dolls and had centre-parted long blonde hair, came with a simple walking action, where the arms and legs would swing in harmony when the doll was made to 'walk', and was taller at 15"/38cm tall. Daisy Long Legs had her own range of Mary Quant designed clothes and wore platform shoes.

Daisy was advertised as 'Daisy the Best Dressed Doll in the World', and there was an extensive range of designer fashion clothes available for the 9"/23cm Daisy dolls. Some of the loveliest of these creations were as follows:

'Bye Bye Baby' check trousers and scarf with royal blue jacket.
'Moulin Rouge' red coat, boots and beret.
'Cucumber Sandwich' long green floral dress.
'Sister Kate' purple flapper dress.
'Neat Pleats' white pleated skirt ensemble.
'Snug Bug' red nightie.
'Shepherds Pie' mauve gingham smock and hat.
'Tea Dance' lemon handkerchief skirt dress.
'Jive' red pleated dress.
'Liquorice Allsorts' multi-coloured horizontal striped dress.
'Fox Trot' red swinging dress.
'Rio' red culottes dress.
'Raindrops' spotted and patterned mini dress.
'Genevieve' purple trouser suit.
'Picnic' red spot dress with over pinny.
'Five O' floral sundress.
'Denimgrad' mauve halter-neck sundress.
'Hoedown' multi-coloured country style tiered dress.
'Jane' suede trousers and leopard skin tunic.
'Miranda' floral maxi dress.
'Mustard' canary yellow coat.
'Pocahontas' patterned kaftan.
'Marlene' pink trouser ensemble.
'Pink Champagne' long, pink frilly dress.
'Heyday' dark floral and striped long dress.
'Promenade' off white pleated dress.
'Arizona' jeans and bra top.
'Sugar Almond' pale-blue wraparound dress.
'Mississippi' striped braced trousers and check top.
'Folderols' pale blue swirl dress.
'Apple Pie' red check maxi wraparound dress.
'Mardi Gras' red top with striped trousers gathered at ankles.
'Sherlock' green plaid coat.
'Tiffany' black and gold dance dress.
'Cuddles' white and tan jerkin and boots.

More beautiful designer fashions were issued in the late Seventies for 'Career Girl' Daisy with four booklets describing them, entitled My Exciting Life as a Reporter, My Gift Shop, My Round the World Holiday and I'm having Fun as at Travel Courier. These fashions included two outfits for visiting each of fourteen countries around the world . The holiday leaflet also depicted a suitcase set called 'Intercity'. A 'Career Girl' set, which included a typewriter, television and telephone, and a 'Top of the Pops' set, including a guitar, posters and drinks tray, were also available. The holiday clothes worn while Daisy was 'packing' were: 'Humbug', a diagonal striped skirt; 'Sunstroke', a vertical striped top; 'Orange Sundae' satin pants; and 'Hornpipe' horizontal-striped pants.

Daisy's around the world outfits were as follows:

For Paris:
'Black Magic' black satin and lace evening dress.
'Able Seaman' black and white separates.

For Denmark:
'Flossie' and 'Hotdog', a pink, furry jacket and red pleated long skirt.
'Sunday Best', a royal blue trench coat with red accessories.

For Moscow:
'Miss Muffet' pink gingham dress, pinny and scarf.
'Hoity Toity' white fur coat and hat.

For India:
'Daddy's Girl' blue gingham dress and hat.
'Flamenco' patterned rouched top and long skirt.

For Japan:
'Knickerbocker Glory' long horizontal striped cotton dress.
'Captain's Table' yellow satin culottes.

For Hong Kong:
'Concorde' red spotted blouse and white pleated skirt.
'Puddleduck' white P.V.C. raincoat and sou'wester trimmed in red.

For Australia:
'Garden Party' pink silky mini dress.
'Posh' blue satin battle dress.

For Tahiti:
'Daisy Chain' frilly dress in daisy print.
'Ring a Roses' blue denim sun-top and long skirt.
'Charleston' red taffeta shimmy dress.

For New York:
'Naughty' pink nightie and black negligee.
'Blossom' pink baby-doll nightie.
'Flapper' and 'Sherbert', spotted cotton top and red satin trousers.
'Confetti' white satin wedding dress.

For Morocco:
'Tango' navy culottes.
'Romany' red spotted sun top and wraparound skirt.

For Egypt:
'Casbah' floral kaftan.
'Banana Split' striped mini dress.
'Signal' red, white and navy trouser suit.

For Greece:
'Smarty' navy and white spot mini dress.
'Cowslip' flowered, co-ordinating top and long skirt.

For Venice:
'Princess' black satin evening dress and red, hooded cloak.
'Peach' denim and lace trouser, top and hat, plus bag.

For London:
'Bees Knees' horizontal striped trouser suit.
'Derby Day' pink taffeta hat, coat and dress with feather trim.
'April Showers' navy taffeta dress and red P.V.C. raincoat.
'St Tropez' frilly, shirred and flowered separates.
'Dotty' spotted red muslin mini dress.
'Wedding Bells' white satin wedding dress.

As well as her beautiful and extensive wardrobe of fashions, Daisy had a red riding jacket and breeches to wear while riding her horse, Archie. There were also things for her home, including: a bedroom suite, comprising a brass bed, pillow and covers; a double-door wooden look plastic wardrobe with drawer space; a dressing table in wood-effect plastic, plus a padded stool and a mirror; a pink, upholstered chaise lounge with dressing mirror and hat stand; a leather-look button-back armchair, side table and lamp; a white, circular dining table and four swivel chairs; and a bean-bag sofa, chairs and pouffe with TV, record player and telephone. In addition, there was a caravan for Daisy, a blue bicycle with rotating pedals and wheels, and a carry case, which held a Daisy doll and a few of her clothes.

★Several wedding dresses were issued for Daisy over the years, but never a groom!

Daisy was marked '© Model Toys' on her seat. In 1980, the doll, sold all over Europe by the Flair Toys franchise, was sold to Harbutts Plasticene Ltd, and promoted by them for only a few years before being discontinued in 1983.

Flair Toys also made two more dolls, available for a couple of years in the mid-Seventies – the Quant Kids, again designed by Mary Quant. 'Bubbles' was a $7\frac{1}{2}$"/19cm sister to Daisy, with short, fair rooted hair in a straight bobbed 'Quant' style, while 'Squeak', her 5"/12.5cm little brother with moulded, brown hair. These dolls' wore the typical children's fashions of the day – from dungarees to party wear in attractive colours and fabrics. Both were marked '© Model Toys Ltd'

In 1976, the company also began promoting another 9"/23cm doll in the Daisy mould, called Havoc Secret Agent, with short flicked-up straight, rooted dark-brown hair and green painted eyes. She was meant to resemble Diana Rigg as her character in the Avengers TV series. The doll had flexible hands (so she could hold a weapon) and wore a zipped navy blue jumpsuit and white boots. A few accessories were also made for her.

Standard Daisy
Model Toys Ltd
9"/23cm
'MCModel Toys Ltd'
1972
This Standard Daisy, wears 'Bees Knees' and is shown in her original box with booklet depicting all the outfits available for Daisy's Round the World Holiday.

Dizzy Daisy
Model Toys Ltd
9"/23cm
'Model Toys Ltd'
1974
Dizzy Daisy was a budget-priced version with non-bending limbs and straight waist. She's wearing the 'Hoedown' outfit of gingham halter-neck and three-tiered skirt in three colourways, from the 'I'm having Fun as a Travel Courier' range.

Daisy Long Legs
Model Toys Ltd
15"/38cm
no markings
1979

An attractive, larger Daisy with similar features to her smaller counterpart and with the added attraction of a walking feature. Pictured in her original box and outfit – a pink off the shoulder long frilly gown called 'Razzamattazz' No 65400, which was also available in blue. Through the bottom window on the box can be seen an attractive free Daisy Long Legs Badge for the child to wear.

Right: The reverse of the Daisy Long Legs box showing six more fashion outfits entitled: 65410 Buster; 65411 Maxims; 65412 Checkmate; 65413 Alibaba; 65414 Follies; and 65415 Sugarpipe. These outfits were available boxed separately for the doll.

Daisy Long Legs (back row), Dizzy Daisy (front left), Brunette Daisy (front centre) Amy (front right)
Model Toys Ltd
Model Toys
1974

Group of Daisy dolls (and Daisy's friend, Amy), showing the harder to find brunette Daisy and brunette Amy.

Daisy's wood-look plastic Wardrobe pictured with its original box and the 'Cucumber Sandwich' outfit pictured on the box. The Standard Daisy doll pictured is wearing a yellow 'May Ball' outfit from the My exciting Life as a Reporter' range.

Dashing Daisy
Model Toys Ltd
9''/23cm
'© Model Toys Ltd'
1975
On the left, Dashing Daisy in 'Ballerina', a lovely three-tone lilac tutu and tights with ballet shoes. On the right, Dashing Daisy in a swimsuit. The dolls are shown posing on their original stands.

Standard Daisy
Model Toys Ltd
9''/23cm
'© Model Toys Ltd'
1972
On the left, the dress from 'April Showers'.
On the right, 'May Ball' outfit in yellow spot and floral.

Standard Daisy
Model Toys Ltd
9''/23cm
'© Model Toys Ltd'
1972
Two Standard Daisy dolls with voluminous curly hair. On the left, wearing a floral dress; on the right, wearing 'Tango', a navy culottes dress. The dolls are pictured posing on their original stands.

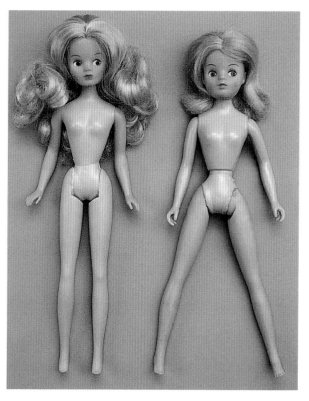

Naked Dashing Daisy (on the left) had swivel jointed hips to enable her to do ballet movements and sit astride her horse, whereas Standard Daisy had only movable legs. Both dolls have flexible arms and knees with six movable joints.

Standard Daisy
Model Toys Ltd
9"/23cm
'© Model Toys Ltd'
1972

On the left, with her hair plaited and wearing 'Liquorice Allsorts'. On the right, wearing 'Air Hostess'. Notice the platform shoes, so typical of the early Seventies fashions. Both outfits from the 'My Exciting Life as a Reporter' range. The dolls are pictured posing on their original stands.

Dashing Daisy on her horse 'Archie'. Dashing Daisy had more flexible limbs and swivel jointed legs to enable to her to sit astride this horse. A Riding Outfit was available for Daisy – not illustrated.

*Daisy's 'Round the World Holiday'
fashion booklet.*

*Two pages from the 'Round
the World Holiday' fashion
booklet, depicting the fashions
for Australia (on the left) and
Tahiti (on the right).*

*Two more pages from the
'Round the World Holiday
Fashion Booklet', this time
depicting the fashions for
Morocco and Egypt.*

Three bubble-packed Daisy outfits, left to right: 'Cucumber Sandwich', 'Kate' and 'Hoedown'.

Three bubble-packed Daisy outfits left to right: 'Bo Peep', 'Sherlock' and 'Moulin Rouge'.

The reverse of a fashion outfit bubble-pack depicting some of the range of items available for Daisy. Notice the bedroom and sitting room furniture illustrated on the pack.

Bubbles and Squeak
Model Toys Ltd
Sizes 7½"/19cm and 5"/12.5cm
'© Model Toys Ltd'
mid Seventies
On the left, little brother Squeak with moulded hair and five joints – he had a squeaker in his body. Big sister Bubbles had fair, straight rooted hair, five joints and some attractive outfits designed for her by Mary Quant.

Disco Girls – Britt
Matchbox/Lesney Products Co Ltd
9''/24cm
'Made in Hong Kong © Hasbro U.S. Pat. Pend'
1973/74
Britt is seen wearing 'Disco Bride' from Boutique 3, shown with Disco Girls Catalogue.

DISCO GIRLS (Matchbox, 1973)

The early Seventies 'disco era' was the influence behind the Disco Girls, Matchbox's take on the teenage doll. Four 9"/24cm teenage girls – a blonde called Britt, with long straight hair and blue eyes; a redhead called Dee, with short curly hair and amber eyes; a brunette called Tia, with long bouncy curls and brown eyes; and a black girl with short curly afro hair called Domino. The four girls had a similar face and painted eyes, but Britt and Tia had a smiling mouth with a white line denoting teeth while Dee and Domino had a closed-lips style smiling mouth. All the dolls had rooted hair, six movable joints (including a twisting waist), action-grip hands and flexible knee-joints, which enabled them, to 'dance' and sit realistically. They were marked 'Made in Hong Kong © Hasbro U.S. Pat. Pend.' across their seats and came in cellophane-windowed boxes wearing differently coloured tunics and toning knee-length boots.

During the first year of production, 'Bride', 'Air Hostess', 'Nurse' and 'Horse Riding' outfits were also produced for the dolls. In the following year, the dolls were available boxed and dressed as 'Disco Bride', 'Freak Out', 'Disco Dancing' and 'Disco Date'; trendy disco gear was also introduced for them, including thirty six outfits, grouped into three 'Boutique' ranges, as follows:

Boutique 1:
'Toodles' short skirt and top.
'Pinkle' pink floral dress.
'Ric-Rac' lemon gingham dress trimmed with blue ric-rac braid.
'Smash Hit' white pleated dress.
'Popsy Pink' pale pink hot-pants.
'Troody Blues' pale blue dress trimmed in red.
'Strawberry Fair' long, patterned red dress.
'Hopscotch' yellow and pink squared long dress.
'Day Out' red plaid coat.

Boutique 2:
'Rockin Jeans' denim jumpsuit.
'Orange Blossom' orange, patterned long skirt and bolero top.
'Sandpiper' sand coloured fur trimmed evening coat.
'Sun Flower' long, yellow dress and patterned cape.
'Cool Flower' long, pale blue frilly dress.
'Smooth Mover' shocking pink culottes jumpsuit.
'Popsy Whopsy' orange hot-pants and green blouse.
'Hot shot' blue trouser suit trimmed with red spot.
'Nickleodian' silver evening trousers and purple top.
'Ragtime' spotted knee breeches and red/yellow jacket.

Disco Girls 'Carrying Case' (1974), taken from the Disco Girls catalogue.

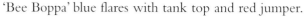

Disco Girls – Britt and Tia

Matchbox/Lesney Products Co Ltd
Sizes: 9"/24cm
'Made in Hong Kong © Hasbro U.S. Pat. Pend'
Left, Britt wearing 'California Campus' from
Boutique 3. Right, Tia wearing 'Ric Rac' from
Boutique 1.

Disco Girls – Domino

Matchbox/Lesney Products Co Ltd
Size 9"/24cm
'Made in Hong Kong © Hasbro U.S. Pat Pending'
1973/74
Domino is seen wearing 'Toodles' from the
Boutique 1 collection – a short red/white striped
skirt and yellow top, red belt and white boots.

Disco Teen – Tony

Matchbox/Lesney Products Co Ltd
9"/24cm
'Made in Hong Kong © Hasbro U.S. Pat Pending,'
1974
Tony is depicted wearing his original outfit and
has rooted dark brown hair with painted features.

'Bee Boppa' blue flares with tank top and red jumper.
'Chatterbox' multi-striped jumpsuit.
'Easy Rider' blue jeans and red suede fringed jerkin and cowboy boots.
'Lazy Lilac' mauve top with toning, checked flared trousers.
'Smartie Pants' maroon flared trousers with striped knit cardigan.
'Summer Time' gingham, long dress and scarf.
'Swinging Suede' beige trousers and suede jerkin over a jumper.
'Rainy Day' shiny yellow and red raincoat and red boots.

Boutique 3:
'Autumn Scene' lurex trousers and hipster coat.
'Honky Tonk' yellow flared trousers and checked bolero, cap and scarf.
'Candy Floss' lilac checked evening dress with purple lace trim.
'California Campus' white flared trousers with red top and blouse.
'Carnival' multi-coloured long dress with front eyelet ties.

In addition to the Boutique clothes, the following four outfits were available both as boxed doll-and-outfit sets and as separately packed outfit sets:

'Disco Bride' long, white lace and button trimmed bridal gown, headdress and veil.
'Disco Dancing' cream tiered long maid of honour style dress with matching picture hat.
'Disco Date' tan, suede trousers with blouse and patterned jerkin.
'Freak Out' white, flared trousers and bolero with purple blouse.

In 1974, friend Tony was introduced with the same 6 moving joints and rooted hair as the girls. He also measured 9"/24cm tall and had dark-brown shoulder-length hair and brown painted eyes. He was packaged in a cellophane-windowed box and came wearing flared denim trousers and an orange sweater. In addition, there were three separate outfits for him: 'Woodstock', a blue denim jumpsuit; 'Nashville', multi striped flared trousers, white shirt and yellow tank top; and 'Jack Flash' white shirt with purple satin trousers with silver flash down the leg seam.

The five 'Disco' dolls and their fashion clothes could be carried in their own 'Carrying Case', issued in 1974 with the same design as appeared on the doll's boxes – a disco theme in vibrant shades of orange, pink and mauve.

The reverse of Tony's box, showing all five of the
Disco Teens – Tony, Domino, Britt, Tia and Dee –
plus three outfits for Tony (Woodstock, Nashville and
Jack Flash).

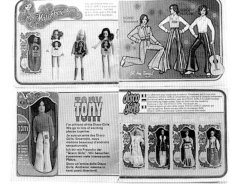

Pages from the Disco Girls catalogue.
Top left: the four Disco Girls – Domino, Dee, Britt and Tia. Below them is Tony, a disco friend introduced in 1974.
Above right: Tony's fashion outfits – Woodstock, Nashville and Jack Flash. Below left: boxed Disco Girls for 1974 – Disco Bride, Freak Out, Disco Darling and Disco Date.

Two pages of Boutique Fashions from the Disco Girls catalogue, depicting 'Troody Blues', 'Strawberry Fair', 'Hopscotch' from Boutique 1; 'Disco Bride' and 'Disco Darling' from Boutique 3; and 'Popsy Whopsy', 'Hot Shot', 'Nickleodian', 'Ragtime', 'Bee Bopa' and 'Chatterbox' from Boutique 2.

Disco Girls from the 1980 Matchbox Catalogue, showing auburn haired Dee wearing 'Disco Rider', blonde haired Britt wearing 'Disco Bride', brunette haired Tia wearing 'Highland Fling', and another brunette haired Tia, this time wearing 'Air Hostess'.

Dolly Darlings
Palitoy
$4\frac{1}{2}$"/11.5cm
'© 1965 Hasbro ®'
1966
A group of Dolly Darlings, showing the varied hairstyles and colours that were available as well as the attractive fashion colours that each one came dressed in.

Dolly Darlings
Palitoy
$4\frac{1}{2}$"/11.5cm
'© 1965 Hasbro ®'
1966
Another group of Dolly Darlings, depicting the lovely fashions available plus more hairstyles and colours.

DOLLY DARLINGS (Palitoy, 1966)

Described in the catalogues as 'the quick selling collector's doll', Dolly Darlings had more of a pre-teen look; but, like the older-looking dolls covered in this book, she came with many different outfits to collect, and all at pocket-money prices. The dolls had rooted hair in many different styles (short, long, curly, ringlets, plaits, ponytail etc) and shades, including pale blonde, fair, auburn, red, light brown, dark brown and black. The doll measured $4\frac{1}{2}$"/11.5cm tall and had painted eyes, painted features and painted on shoes or boots. In all, there was a wide range of eye- and shoe-colour combinations. The earlier models had straight waists, while those introduced in 1967 had twisting waists, and all had fully-jointed limbs with attractively sculptured and posed hands.

The dolls came boxed with their own little brush and comb. The outfits came with names such as 'Powder Puff', 'Sweetheart', 'Honey', 'Lemon Drop', 'Sunny Day', 'Dream', 'Party' and 'Schoolgirl', and included trouser suits, day dresses, party dresses, skirts and blouses, jumpers and jerkins, fur trimmed coats and hats, raincoats and hats, school uniforms, nurses outfit, a Scottish kilt, nightwear, swimwear, bikinis and underwear. Dolly Darlings were marked '© 1965 Hasbro ®' across the shoulders. Later dolls were marked in the same way with 1967 as their date, and the dolls were available for almost ten years. Today, they are very popular collector's items, as a large and varied collection can be built up without it taking up very much space.

Dolly Darlings
Palitoy
$4\frac{1}{2}$"/11.5cm
'© 1965 Hasbro ®'
1966
This popular outfit was called 'Tea Time' and also came in navy and white.

Pennies
Palitoy
6"/12cm
'Penny Cute © Perfecta Hong Kong'
1969
*Cute little pre-teen dolls at pocket-money prices
with removable clothes, rooted hair and painted
features.*

PENNIES (Palitoy, 1969)

Pennies were made by Palitoy at the same time as Dolly Darlings. The series of six 'little girl' dolls were 6"/12cm tall with cute faces and were marked 'Penny Cute © Perfecta Hong Kong' on the back of the head. Pennies had short, fringed centre-parted rooted hair in blonde, fair, auburn and brown, painted smiling faces with round black dot eyes and jointed limbs. They also had their own range of clothes and were sold at pocket-money prices – hence the name, 'Pennies'. Pennies were only made for a little over a year and today they are harder to find than Dolly Darlings.

PEN PALS (Palitoy, 1970)

Another pocket-money range from Palitoy was Pen Pals. Available for two years in the early Seventies, these 5"/13cm teenage-style jointed dolls were sold in authentic national costumes from around the world. They had rooted hair in a range of style and colours to suit the region from which they 'came'. The dolls were packaged in book-style boxes bearing the appropriate country's national flag. As well as a being dressed in authentic costumes, each doll came with a map and leaflet describing the customs of its country. The range was divided into two series. Series 1 came in a blue pack and consisted of Eskimo, Indian, Spanish, Japanese, Dutch, Welsh, Hawaiian, Mexican and Irish dolls. Series 2 came in a red pack and consisted of Persian, Danish, Arabian, German, Burmese, Red Indian, Chinese and Scottish dolls.
If six dolls were bought at one time, a free 'Bookcase' was included to store the dolls in their packs. Alternatively, six tokens could be collected and the Bookcase, which held twelve packs, could then be redeemed.

CHELSEA GIRL (Palitoy, 1972)

Introduced for one year only, these pocket-money teenage dolls were $11\frac{1}{2}$" /29cm tall with a long side-parted no-fringe hairstyle in blonde or brunette. They came with six different outfits – short dresses and hot-pants in bright colours and patterns – with a further eight outfits available separately in similar styles. The dolls were packed in cellophane bags with a brightly coloured header card to attract the impulse purchase.

Dusty
Denys Fisher
11½"/29cm
'© GMFGI' (the initials of the General Mills Fun
Group Inc)
1976
Dusty the British Airways Jet Setting Stewardess,
pictured in her original outfit and standing next to
her box with original leaflet.

DUSTY (Denys Fisher, 1976)

First introduced in 1974 by Kenner in the U.S.A., tennis-girl Dusty hit the shops at a time when tennis champion Billie Jean King was at the height of her career. The doll had a tennis buddy, black friend 'Skye'. By 1978, however, 'Darci' the cover girl, top fashion model 'Erica' and black friend 'Dana' had replaced Dusty and Skye in popularity in the U.S.A.

Dusty arrived on the British market in 1976 under licence to Denys Fisher (which, like Kenner, was by then owned by General Mills Inc). She was boxed with a leaflet describing her as 'Dusty the British Airways Jet Setting Stewardess', travelling the world to many exotic places'. She measured $11\frac{1}{2}$" /29cm tall and was a suntanned, outdoors kind of girl, with stylish, short pale-blonde hair, sparkling blue eyes and a lovely smiling mouth with pastel lips. Her robust vinyl body was fully jointed, with flexible limbs, including wrists and a swivelling twist waist. She came boxed in a stewardess uniform in navy and red. Several lovely boxed trendsetter outfits reflecting Seventies fashions were available for this doll, to help her join in with local activities wherever she travelled. Dusty could have fun in Hawaii dressed in a multi floral bikini, natural grass skirt and garlands; she took her surfboard and guitar along too. A traditional cream floral kimono and sandals came in handy in Japan with a fan and parasol. In Switzerland, Dusty could go ski-ing in a very chic yellow jumper and red dungarees outfit with matching yellow ski boots, red skis and sticks. While on safari in Africa, Dusty could wear her beige linen safari suit and film and view the animals with a camera and binoculars.

Another range of Dusty dolls was 'Sporting Dusty and Real Action Sports Doll'. 'Swimming Champ' was wearing a navy swimming costume and flat shoes. (This and all the sporting outfits had the tiny white daisy motif stitched to them.) 'Soft Ball Champ' was wearing pink shorts and cap with a green top and lace-up shoes, stand, bat and ball. 'Golf Champ' came wearing a pink checked skirt and white top with pink-and-white shoes, stand, golf club and balls. 'Tennis Champ' was wearing a white tennis dress trimmed with green daisies, green-and-white shoes, stand, racket and ball. And 'Volley Ball Champ' came wearing yellow shorts, top and shoes, stand and ball. These sets were available as boxed dressed dolls or as separately boxed outfits.

In addition to these sets, there was 'Award Night' set, which included a Dusty doll in a Gold Evening Gown with presentation trophy and two sports outfits: Tennis Champ and Golf Champ.

real action
ts-doll...
suntanned
loor

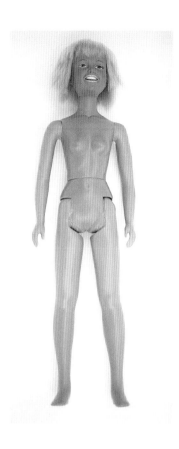

In 1976, Denys Fisher ran a competition for children of fourteen years and under to 'Design a "Holiday" Costume' for Dusty to wear on her travels. The prize was a day out at the British Airways Cabin Crew Training School. By 1977, Dusty had been discontinued.

She was marked '© GMFGI' (the initials of General Mills Fun Group Inc).

Dusty
Denys Fisher
11½"/29cm
'© CMFGI'
Dusty the Golf Champ, pictured in front of her box and wearing pink checked skirt, white top and pink and white shoes, and shown with her stand, golf club and ball. Notice the other outfits depicted on the reverse of the box.

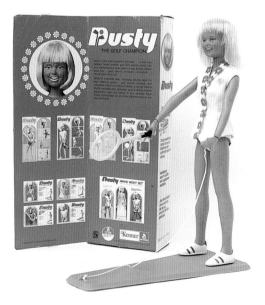

Dusty
Denys Fisher
11½"/29cm
'© CMFGI'
1976
Dusty the Tennis Champ, pictured in front of her box wearing white tennis dress and pants, green and white shoes, and shown with her stand, racquet and ball.

Taken from the leaflet found inside the box in illustration (134) and showing the four outfits available for Dusty's jet setting lifestyle.

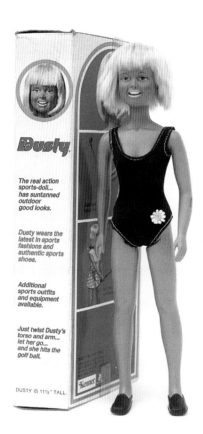

One of the boxed jet setting outfits available for Dusty, called 'Dusty in Africa'. (136)

Dusty
Denys Fisher
$11\frac{1}{2}$"/29cm
'© CMFGI'
1976
Dusty the Swimming Champ, wearing navy swimsuit and slip on shoes. All the Dusty fashions had the tiny daisy detail.

*Illustration from Pedigree's 1977
catalogue showing the three Fairy Tale
Teens, from left to right: Snow White,
Cinderella and Alice in Wonderland.*

FAIRY TALE TEENS (Pedigree, 1978)

During the early- to mid-Fifties, Walt Disney made cartoon films of children's stories such as 'Alice in Wonderland', 'Snow White' and 'Cinderella'. These films were huge box-office attractions and the usual promotional items and toys followed including T-shirts, mugs, stationery, jigsaws, pottery figures – and dolls.

In the late Seventies, Pedigree produced a series of Walt Disney favourites: Alice in Wonderland, Snow White and Cinderella were faithfully reproduced from the early Disney films and are recognisable in their costumes. Alice in Wonderland had long, blonde rooted centre-parted hair with an alice band holding it back from her face. Her dress was cornflower blue with a long skirt covered by a white pinafore Snow White had wavy centre-parted brown rooted hair, and a yellow and blue dress with a red cape. Cinderella had short, curly blonde rooted hair in an upswept top-knot style and came wearing a two-tone pale-blue ballgown.

The dolls themselves were poseable vinyl teenage dolls not unlike Sindy. They were $11\frac{1}{2}$"/29cm tall with similar faces, painted large, blue side-glancing eyes with eye lashes and a wide smile with slightly rosy cheeks – and Alice had a few freckles over her nose. They bore no identifying marks and without their clothes are difficult to identify.

An illustration showing the naked bodies of the Fairy Tale Teens. They closely resemble the Sindy bodies of the same period, with six joints and flexible limbs.

Alice in Wonderland
Snow White
Cinderella
Pedigree
11½"/29cm
no markings
1978
The three Pedigree Walt Disney Fairy Tale Teens, left to right: Alice in Wonderland, Snow White and Cinderella. All dressed in faithful reproduction of the outfits in the early Walt Disney cartoon films.

FARRAH (Airfix, 1977) and SUPERSTAR (Palitoy, 1977)

Both of these beautiful, 13"/33cm tall dolls were marked across the small of the back '© Mego Corporation 1975 Made in Hong Kong'. They had identical bodies with extremely long flexible limbs, jointed heads, waists, legs and arms with long slender fingers and moulded finger nails.

Farrah was a glamorous superstar with painted green eyes and long eyelashes and a super smile. Her strawberry-blonde shoulder-length hair had the famous bouncy wavy flicked-back style of actress Farrah Fawcett as she appeared in the television programme Charlie's Angels running at that time. She came boxed wearing a white halter-neck jumpsuit and white heeled shoes. Several more outfits were available for her reminiscent of the outfits her character wore in the TV programme. Knitting patterns were also available at the time, depicting the doll in long, sleek designs.

In addition to the general mark on the small of her back, this doll was marked '© Farrah' on the back of her neck.

Superstar had painted blue eyes with long eyelashes and a similar super smile to Farrah. Her pale blonde hip-length rooted hair was straight and centre parted. Described as 'the doll with the style of her own', she had three fantastic fashion collections: 'Star Collection', 'Starglow Collection' and 'Stardust Collection'. Each collection comprised six outfits, all with the same long, glamorous sparkling evening-dress theme, plus accessories and culottes or flared trousers with stoles. Each collection came with high-heeled shoes in colours to match the outfits. Superstar came wearing a silver lurex halter-neck evening dress in a box decorated with a city scene. On the reverse were pictures of some of the additional outfits available for her. Palitoy operated a 'star' collection scheme, whereby a child could collect stars printed on the boxes and redeem them for a free Superstar outfit that was not available in any store.

Superstar's clothes were unmarked and the doll had only the general '© Mego Corporation 1975 Made in Hong Kong' mark across the small of the back.

Farrah
Airfix
13"/33cm
'© Mego Corporation 1975 Made in Hong Kong'
1977
Farrah is photographed in front of a knitting pattern booklet that featured several lovely styles to knit for this doll.

doll's fashion 543

Patterns for all occasions

Farrah
Airfix
13"/33cm
'© Mego Corporation 1975 Made in Hong Kong'
1977
This Farrah wears a knitted dress taken from the knitting pattern book behind her. Several boxed outfits were also available for this glamorous doll.

Superstar
Palitoy
13"/33cm
© Mego Corporation 1975
1977
*Super Star pictured with her box which states
"She'll go far dressed like a Star". Some of the
Superstar fashions are pictured on her box.
(Collection: Christine Wimsey: Photo by Phil)*

*One of the Superstar outfits available for the doll
in illustration together with more fashions pictured
on the reverse of the bubble packs.*

Miss Amanda Jane
Amanda Jane
$7\frac{1}{2}$"/19cm
Miss Amanda Jane
1979
This blonde Miss Amanda Jane wears
'Co-ordinate Print Dress & Purse' one of the
lovely boxed outfits that were available for her.

MISS AMANDA JANE
(Amanda Jane/Pemmary Designs, 1979)

Sophisticated, fashion-conscious Miss Amanda Jane was a sweet pre-teen doll measuring $7\frac{1}{2}$"/19cm, with rooted blonde or brunette hair in a side-parted wavy shoulder-length style, painted brown eyes and a shy smile. Her fully jointed body had a twist waist and she was introduced wearing a tiny floral-print dress in creamy beige with cream mesh tights and grey shoes. Five additional outfits were available for her packed separately: a flowery apricot lawn two-piece suit, a cream nightdress and dressing-gown, a grey/beige print dress and purse, a weekend-set of beige corduroy trousers and check shirt, and a pastel-green dinner gown and stole.

By 1980, many more outfits were added to Miss Amanda Jane's range. She now came boxed and dressed in a blue or red check sundress, and the new additional outfits for her included: a floral two-piece suit with white blouse; a white undies set; a jumpsuit in shocking pink/yellow glazed cotton; a long, floral pastel dress and pinny; blue jeans, check blouse and anorak; shocking pink culottes-style disco set; Bermuda shorts, blouse, sun visor and shoulder bag; red tights and stripy knit dress; and a little red duffle coat that could top them all. Accessories were also introduced at this time and included a beautiful bed with blue floral covers.

A Miss Amanda Jane bride doll was also introduced in 1980, presented in her own transparent reusable plastic box; she wore a lovely white silky self-patterned two tier bridal gown with short sleeves and bow detail on the bodice and a fine white net veil, which was held in place with a ribbon rosette, and she carried a posy of blue forget-me-knot flowers. Her half slip and panties were of white nylon.

In addition, the child could collect the Amanda Jane signatures printed on the packaging; when twelve had been collected they could be sent off in exchange for a new surprise outfit.

The dolls were marked across the shoulders 'Miss Amanda Jane' in signature form.

Clockwise, from above:

Miss Amanda Jane
Amanda Jane
$7\frac{1}{2}$"/19cm
Miss Amanda Jane
1979
On the left a brunette wearing 'Disco Set' and on the right: a blonde wearing 'Dinner Gown & Stole'. Both outfits were available boxed for this doll.

Miss Amanda Jane
Amanda Jane
$7\frac{1}{2}$"/19cm
Miss Amanda Jane
1979
These two Miss Amanda Janes are wearing: on the left: 'Flowered Apricot Lawn Two Piece' and on the right: 'Weekend Set'. Both outfits were available boxed for this doll.

Miss Amanda Jane
Amanda Jane
$7\frac{1}{2}$"/19cm
Miss Amanda Jane
1980
Miss Amanda Jane Bride was introduced in 1980 and came complete in a transparent re-usable plastic box.

Miss Amanda Jane

The very pretty and more sophisticated Miss Amanda Jane doll (19cm high) has great appeal for the fashion conscious little girl. Jeans, Jump Suit and Disco outfit are just a few of the exciting outfits available and illustrated above.

Code colour for all the packs for the Miss Amanda Jane range is Cinnamon Brown.

La très jolie poupée Miss Amanda Jane (19 cm de long), qui est plus sophistiquée, est très appréciée des petites filles que la mode intéresse. Jeans, combinaisons et tenue pour le disco ne sont que quelques-uns des ensembles ravissants pour l'habiller qui sont illustrés ci-dessus.

Le code couleur de chaque emballage de la gamme Miss Amanda Jane est brun clair.

Diese entzückende, und etwas elegantere Miss Amanda Jane Puppe (19cm hoch) erfreut sich ganz besonders bei modebewußten kleinen Mädchen großer Beliebtheit. Jeans, Jump-Suit und Disco-Outfit sind nur einige der aufregenden Ensembles, die für diese Puppe erhältlich sind, siehe obige Abbildung.

Codefarbe für die Miss Amanda Jane Serie ist Zimtbraun.

AMANDA JANE LIMITED, HALFWAY BRIDGE, PETWORTH, WEST SUSSEX. GU28 9BS, ENGLAND.
Telephone: (079-85) 361. Cables: Amandafun Lodsworth.

Left:
Leaflet available in 1980 showing the updated items and fashions available for Miss Amanda Jane.

Above:
An Amanda Jane leaflet showing the early outfits available for the Miss Amanda Jane dolls in 1979.

Miss Amanda Jane shown naked. She had six joints including a twist waist. Painted eyes and rooted hair in blonde or brunette.

This illustration shows the Miss Amanda Jane signature style trademark that appeared on these lovely little dolls.

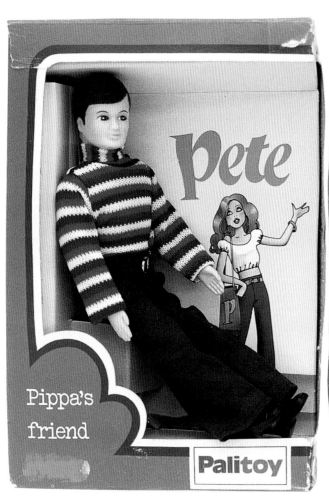

Pippa & Pete
Palitoy
$6\frac{1}{2}$"/17cm
Palitoy Hong Kong
Pippa 1972 – Pete 1974
This illustration shows Pippa in her box on the right and friend
Pete on the left sitting in his original box.

PIPPA, PETE AND FRIENDS (Palitoy, 1972)

Pippa was a 6 $\frac{1}{2}$"/17cm vinyl fully poseable doll that could be used as a dolls-house doll being of similar size to the $\frac{1}{12}$ th scale models available for this purpose at the time (although she also had a flat pack apartment of her own). She had eight movable joints (head, arms, waist, legs and metal-pin jointed knees), making her look very realistic in many positions, such as sitting in chairs, kneeling by a bed etc. Pippa's painted blue eyes had real eyelashes and her rooted hair was long, straight, fair and centre-parted. She wore an orange trouser suit.

In 1973, Palitoy introduced four 'friends' for Pippa. Marie was a suntanned French friend, with rooted, long centre-parted brown hair and brown painted eyes with real eyelashes; she wore a patterned skirt and halter-neck top. Tammie had a pale complexion and long, rooted centre-parted auburn hair and painted blue eyes with real eyelashes; she wore a long, floral dress. Britt was from Scandinavia, was suntanned, had pale-blonde, long centre-parted rooted hair, pale blue painted eyes with real eyelashes, and wore a squared-top ski outfit. Emma had long dark-brown hair and pale complexion, and wore a dress. Although all the friends were presented in their own outfits, they could wear any of the fashions designed for Pippa, as they were the same size as her.

For 1975, three more friends were introduced: a black friend called Mandy, with curly black, rooted hair, dark-brown painted eyes with eyelashes, who wore a red spotted dress; an oriental friend called Jasmine, with long, black glossy centre-parted hair and brown painted eyes; she wore a blue Kimono with embroidered motif; and a white friend, Penny who had a short, auburn curled-up-ends hair style and wore a blue checked dress. At this time, Pippa was boxed in different outfits of daisy-printed frocks.

The following year friend Gail was introduced (with beautiful blonde hair and wearing a long skirt and off-the-shoulder top) along with boyfriend Pete (moulded black hair and painted blue eyes and wearing a multi-striped sweatshirt and navy trousers). Unlike all of Pippa's other friends, Pete had a wardrobe of clothes of his own.

All of Pippa's 'friends' came with the same fully jointed and poseable bodies and were the same size as her, being 6 $\frac{1}{2}$"/17cm tall. They came in cellophane-fronted boxes and were marked 'Palitoy Hong Kong' on their seats.

In 1977 'Dancing Princess Pippa' was introduced, with ankle-length golden-blonde rooted hair and wearing a green evening gown. Along with her came 'Dancing Pippa', 'Dancing Pete', 'Dancing Britt', 'Dancing Marie' and 'Dancing Tammie'. The dolls had the same faces as before, but now came with smooth flexible legs and a 'dancing action' – a rotating arm that caused the doll to swivel at the waist and neck as though dancing.

Many beautiful fashion clothes were made for Pippa, Pete and friends including the named collections 'Paris', 'London', 'New York', 'Rome', 'Geneva', 'Vienna', 'Amsterdam', 'Rio', 'Monaco' and 'Monte Carlo'. Each collection had six different outfits, making over sixty outfits in a wide variety of styles, fabrics and colours. The range included underwear, nightwear, day dresses, evening dresses, casual trousers, skirts and tops, coats and hats, and the uniforms (such as 'Tally Ho', a riding outfit). For 1978, the 'Career Girl' set was introduced, which included 'Nurse', 'Air Stewardess' and 'Secretary'. 'Pippa Goes Dancing' comprised a ballet outfit and black-and-gold ballgown. 'Pippa the Bride' and 'Penny the Bridesmaid' were boxed sets comprising a beautiful all-white lace gown and a peach lace gown for the bridesmaid. Other named collections included 'Kings Road', 'Holidays', 'Mix'n'Match', 'Oriental Collection', 'Pete Collection' and 'Budget Fashions'.

On each of the Pippa and Friends packs were printed flower petals to cut out and collect to make a seven-petal flower; the flower could then be redeemed for a surprise fashion outfit or another new 'friend', Rosemary, who had yellow-blonde long hair and the same size and body as Pippa.

In addition to her regular collection of clothes, Pippa became the owner of a 'Boutique', with several more fashion outfits included in the set. 'Hairdressing Salon' was another new set, with washstand basin and hairdryer. A 'Pony and Gymkhana Set' contained a pony, gates, fences, hedges etc, all made in plastic. 'Pippa's Car' was a sleek red two-seater sports model with chrome trim. A 'Caravan and White Range Rover' came with picnic accessories for more fun.

Pippa's 'Apartment' had been available since 1973, but was updated again in 1978. It was a flat-packed printed-board construction, that was slotted together to form four rooms. Plastic furniture could be purchased separately and included all the usual things, such as a 'Bathroom Suite', 'Kitchen Set', 'Lounge Set', 'Dining Room Set' and accessories such as crockery, cutlery, saucepans – everything to make Pippa's home smart, comfortable and realistic looking.

Pippa's Carry Case, also available since 1973, had a compartment for a doll and hanging space for many outfits. It, too, was updated in 1978.

Pippa & Pete shown nude. The jointed bodies can be clearly seen and are metal pin jointed.

For 1980, Pippa was presented in yet another new floral outfit and newly designed beige packs. New products available at this time included an updated 'Princess Pippa' in an attractive green-and-red braided dress and 'Gala Occasion Pippa' in a new top-quality multi-braided dress and matching braided straw hat. During the ten years that Pippa was in production hundreds of lovely fashion outfits were available for her. She was discontinued in the early Eighties.

Pippa with five boxed outfits and one cellophane carded pocket-money pack. These attractive little outfits were not individually named either on the boxes or in the catalogue, but just named as 'fashion collections'.

Pippa
Palitoy
$6\frac{1}{2}$"/17cm
Palitoy Hong Kong
1974
Shown in her box, Pippa Goes Dancing came with two complete outfits: Ballet tutu and Ballroom gown.

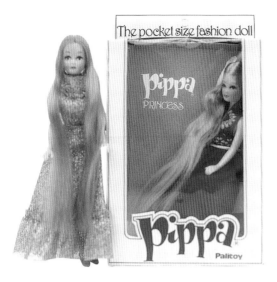

The pocket size fashion doll

Dancing Princess Pippa, on the left, with long, golden, ankle-length straight, rooted hair and wearing her original green and silver lurex evening gown.
On the right, a boxed Princess Pippa with the same long ankle length hair, jointed knees and red evening gown. Both dolls measure $6\frac{1}{2}$"/17cm tall.

Pippa's friend Pete shown with five of his boxed outfits which included trousers, tops, hats and shoes.

Pippa's Career Girl Set is illustrated showing the contents of the box together with the attractive box lid. The set comprised Nurses Uniform with hospital chart. Air Hostess Uniform with refreshment tray and Day Wear with an office typewriter with working platen. Three pairs of shoes were also included in the set.

Pippa's Sport Car 1973 pictured in front of its original box with friend Pete in the Driving Seat and Pippa as his passenger.

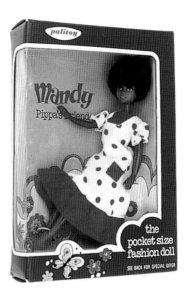

Pippa's friend Jasmine shown mint-in-box, with long sleek glossy black centre parted hair and blue oriental eyes. She came wearing a blue Kimono, 6½"/17cm tall .

Pippa's friend Mandy shown mint-in-box with curly short black rooted hair, black complexion and dark brown painted eyes with eyelashes, 6½"/17cm tall.

Pippa's friend Penny on the left with short curly auburn rooted hair wearing an outfit from the Pippa "Trouser Suits" collection. Tammie another friend with long straight auburn rooted hair is shown mint in box on the right. Both dolls measure 6½"/17cm tall.

Pippa's Carry Case 1973 with hanging space for several outfits and room for Pippa and a friend. The updated 1978 version was bright glossy red with double front openings.

Gail & Pippa
Palitoy
6½"/17cm
Palitoy Hong Kong
1974
On the left Pippa's Bridesmaid Gail with short curly dark brown rooted hair wearing an apricot dress with white chiffon overskirt.
On the right a Pippa Bride wearing a full length white lace bridal gown. Both are mint in box and the detail on the inner box sleeve depicts the occasion.

Pippa
Palitoy
6 ½"/17cm
Palitoy Hong Kong
1974
Pippa's Hair Salon with mirrored sink unit, trolley table with brush, comb, curlers etc and a hairdryer with chair. Pictured are two identical Pippa dolls.

Pippa
Palitoy
6 ½"/17cm
Palitoy Hong Kong
1973
Three separate playsets are illustrated in this Pippa Scene: Pippa in her Riding Outfit, Pippa's Pony, and Pippa's Gymkhana Set which contained gates, fences and hedges.

Pippa, Marie, Tammie, Britt and Mandy
Palitoy
6 ½"/17cm
Palitoy Hong Kong
1973: Black Friend 1974

left to right:
'Pippa' with fair rooted centre parted long hair.
'Marie' her suntanned French friend with brown rooted centre parted long hair.
'Tammie' with auburn rooted centre parted long hair.
'Britt' her Scandinavian friend with suntanned complexion and pale blonde rooted centre parted long hair and Mandy with a black rooted short curly bubble cut style.
All the dolls have painted features and the same fully-jointed posable bodies.

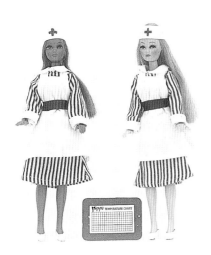

Marie & Pippa
Palitoy
6½"/17cm
Palitoy Hong Kong
1974
*Marie and Pippa in their Nurses'
Uniforms of blue striped dresses
with white collars and cuffs, white
cap, apron and shoes with a
Temperature Chart.*

Pippa, Britt, Pippa
Palitoy
6½"/17cm
Palitoy Hong Kong
1973
*Fashions in Red from the London, Paris and New York
Pippa Fashion Collections.*

Marie, Britt, and Mandy
Palitoy
6½"/17cm
Palitoy Hong Kong
1973

*More outfits from the Pippa Fashion
Collections. On the left a floral dress and
shawl. Centre a red and cream lace creation
and on the right a stunning silver evening
dress and bag.*

Marie, Marie, and Pippa
Palitoy
6½"/17cm
Palitoy Hong Kong
1973
*Three more attractive Pippa outfits
modelled by two Maries on the left and
a Pippa on the right.*

Sindy's 'Carry Case' shown open to reveal hanging space for clothes and section for a Sindy doll. (The 1963 Brunette Sindy shown is wearing 'Winter Holiday'.) The case shown closed reveals the doll peeping out. The child could carry a doll and outfits wherever she went. Introduced in 1967/68 with a square handle. Re-introduced in 1974 with a round handle.

SINDY, PAUL AND FRIENDS (Pedigree, 1963)

Sindy was first introduced in 1963 by Pedigree, a company based in Merton, southwest London. She was designed by one of the company's employees, Dennis Arkinstall, and closely resembled 'Tammy', made by the Ideal Toy Corporation of America and introduced in 1962. Pedigree even used a similar advertising slogan to that of Tammy – 'Sindy, the doll you love to dress' – and some of the packaging was similar, too. Sindy was advertised widely on television and in many teenage magazines in the early Sixties, but no-one then imagined that Sindy would survive four decades and still be selling well in the new millennium. The TV jingle that launched Sindy in the London area on Sunday 6th September 1963 at 6pm went as follows:

Take an S, take an I, take an N, D, Y and
What have you got?
You've got SINDY.
The doll you'll love to dress.

Who is the Belle at every Ball?
Who wears the prettiest dress of them all?
Who is the girly you all love best?
It's SINDY!
The doll you'll love to dress.

Who steals the scene at every show?
Who is the best-dressed girl you know?
Who is the girl they all love best?
It's SINDY!
The doll you'll love to dress.

Who's got a record player, brush and comb?
A little doggie all of her own?
Who is the girl they all love best?
It's SINDY!
The doll you'll love to dress.

The advert, with its catchy jingle, was aired a further 25 times between September 30th and Christmas Day of that year, when the first eight Sindy outfits and eight Sindy separates were also screened, along with Sindy's dog Ringo, her skates and a gramophone player. Sindy, every little girl's dream come true!

Over the last four decades Sindy has modelled a vast wardrobe of different fashions. In the Sixties, her clothes were designed by Art School Students and were largely made of natural fibres (cottons, silks, wools) and modelled on the classics of Hartnell in the Fifties and the modern teenage fashions of the early Sixties, era of The Beatles and Mary Quant. The Seventies saw the mini and midi fashions of the Mary Quant designs and the bright synthetic fabrics of the late Sixties and early Seventies Flower-Power style. The Eighties witnessed designer trends from the Emanuels and Zandra Rhodes, plus new owners and several new faces for Sindy. Houses, complete with furniture, working kitchens and many accessories, also appeared in abundance for Sindy.

Sindy was advertised at the time as being twelve inches tall, but although the first batches certainly were 12"/30cm, later ones were slightly different heights, meaning that all Sindy measurements are approximate. The September 1963 dolls were made from vinyl with slightly bending arms, non-bending vinyl blow-moulded legs and a body with five movable joints (neck, arms and legs). The dolls had hand-painted lips and painted side-glancing blue eyes and were available with blond, auburn or brunette short rooted hair in a wavy style. This first Sindy doll was rather lightweight and marked 'Made in England' on the back of her neck. She was sold boxed and dressed in a 'Weekenders' outfit of blue denim jeans with lime green stitching, a striped top of red, blue and white (although on later on later batches the stripe order is red, white, blue), white plastic casual 'tie' shoes and a red hair band. (The Weekenders outfit was current until 1967.) A doll-stand for posing Sindy and a little booklet were included, describing extra outfits in styles typical of the late Fifties and early Sixties that could be purchased separately. Some of these fashions were depicted on her box. All the early fashions – many produced from 1963 to 1970 – were extremely well-made, with plenty of detailing, such as tiny zips and buttons.
The first few boxed outfits available for Sindy from 1963 were: 'Sleepy-Time', a pink check baby doll nightie; 'Undie-World', a dark-blue nylon slip, bra and panties; 'Dream-Date', a pink party dress; 'Lunch-Date', a navy and green wool dress with tartan skirt; 'Skating-Girl', a red and white skating outfit; 'Shopping-in-the-Rain', a navy plastic trench coast and red boots and bag; 'Pony-Club', a brown riding jacket and beige breeches; 'Country-Walk', a brown suede jacket and tweed skirt; 'Bridesmaid', a lemon chiffon trimmed dress; 'Seaside-Sweetheart', a beach outfit and wrap; 'Winter-Holiday', a ski outfit; 'Emergency-Ward', a nurse's uniform; 'Happy-traveller', a grey wool coat; 'Air-Hostess', a stewardess uniform; 'Centre-Court', a tennis dress with 'S' initial and racket; and 'Bowling', a Bermuda shorts and cardigan. All these attractively boxed outfits came with extra little accessories for longer play value.

Now that Sindy had such an array of beautifully made clothes to wear, a wardrobe and bed were introduced for her and a red two-seater MGB model sports car from 1964 to 1969 with chrome bumpers, hubcaps and headlamps. The car was a realistic scaled model of the classic MGB sports car of the Sixties; the wardrobe was of white plastic with double doors and legs, full length mirror, shelf for hats, shoe racks and drawers for underclothes; and the bed was also of white plastic with a headboard decorated with white cherubs in 'Hollywood' gilded style with frilly white and lemon or white and pink bedspread and sheets. Sindy also had a horse called 'Peanuts' that she could ride and a pony called 'Pixie'. Other furniture introduced through the Sixties included a 'Dressing Table and Stool', 'Bedside Table and Lamp', 'Chest of Drawers', a 'Washday Set', a 'Sink Unit' and 'Bath Unit' that could be filled with water. A 'Kitchen drop-leaf Table and Chairs' in blue plastic was another attractive set and, last but not least, there was a 'Carry-me-Case' introduced for Sindy in 1967, which had space for a doll and hanging space for many items of clothing on tiny hangers. In 1968, the 'Carry-me-Case' was updated to a 'Blue Wardrobe Trunk' for travelling, which also had space for many outfits, as it measured 7" x $3\frac{1}{2}$" x $3\frac{1}{2}$" (18cm x 9cm x 9cm) and came with a sheet of stickers from Sindy's holiday destinations, with which the child could decorate it.

Also available in the Sixties were cut-out paper-doll Sindy books, with an printed card version of Sindy and printed paper copies of her early clothing. Colouring books, jigsaw puzzles, annuals and wallpaper for a child's bedroom all feature the early outfits. There was also a box of miniature chocolates plus a 'pop-record' of the 'Dollybeats' singing group that was made at the height of The Beatles popularity.

In 1965, Sindy was updated. Her head, arms and legs were now made of a more rigid vinyl with wired, slightly bending limbs. She was shorter, at $11\frac{1}{4}$"/28.5cm tall, although different batches came in at $11\frac{1}{2}$"/29cm. She was now referred to as 'Sindy, the Model', because of her extensive wardrobe of clothes. This updated Sindy came dressed in the same 'Weekenders' outfit as before, but had a different, short, thick wavy hairstyle of blonde, auburn or brunette nylon and was altogether much prettier and of better quality than the 1963 version. She had five joints and was marked 'Made in England' on the small of her back, although some batches were not marked at all. Many more clothes were added to her wardrobe at this time, plus a hair switch on an alice band, to give Sindy some glamorous longer hairstyles.

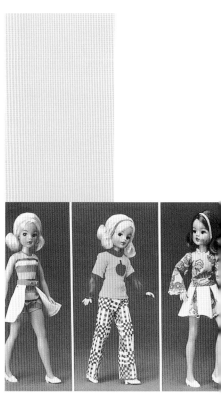

Soon to follow in 1965 was a boyfriend called 'Paul' and a little sister called 'Patch'.

Boyfriend Paul measured $11\frac{3}{4}$"/29.5cm tall, was made of hard vinyl with wired limbs and had five joints. A painted face with brown forward-facing eyes and brown painted moulded hair completed his look. He was marked 'Made in Hong Kong' across his shoulders and he came dressed in a 'Casuals' outfit – that complimented Sindy's 'Weekenders' outfit – of blue jeans and red cotton knit pullover with polo neck and white plastic sneaker shoes. He, too, had a complete wardrobe of fashion clothes, many of which matched or complimented those for Sindy. Paul's box also resembled Sindy's, depicting three further possible outfits.

Little sister Patch was $8\frac{1}{2}$"/21.5cm tall, was in production from 1965 to 1969 and was marked 'Made in Hong Kong' across her shoulders. She was also made from vinyl with wired limbs and five joints, had painted features including blue side-glancing eyes and freckles over her nose. She had short, fringed straight hair in a choice of blonde, auburn or brunette. She came boxed in 'Dungarees', an outfit of blue denim dungarees with red and white checked top, headscarf and checked patch on one knee. The box, like Sindy's and Paul's, depicted the first three outfits available for her.

All the early Sixties outfits for Sindy, Paul and Patch were labelled with a little black on white embroidered cotton label stitched into the back neck or side seam making them easy to identify and attribute. For a complete list of all the early Sindy, Paul and Patch clothes see the end of this chapter.

Patch's American friend Betsy was available from 1967 to 1969, wearing a red cord sleeveless dress trimmed with guipure lace, white panties and shoes, and boxed in a cellophane-fronted pack with a stars and stripes badge. She had painted forward-facing blue eyes, rooted brown or blonde curly hair with a fringe, moving head and fixed flexible wired arms and legs. The doll was tiny at $6\frac{1}{2}$"/17cm tall and was unmarked. Three separate outfits were available for her: 'Sleeptight' nightie; 'Fun and Games' blue check trousers and denim top; and 'Party Time', a pink frilly party dress, bag and floral posy. She also had a poodle dog called 'Hector', with a bowl and bone. (This dog was exactly like Sindy's 1963 pooch 'Ringo'.) All the doll's outfits came with little accessories.

In 1968, Sindy was updated again. This time she had a longer hairstyle with side-parted rooted shoulder length hair, in pale blonde, auburn and brunette. She had the same side-glancing painted blue eyes, but now with long eyelashes. Her body was similar to the previous Sindy, but with a twisting waist and more poseable limbs, with six joints. She was marked 'Made in Hong Kong' on the back of her neck, and she measured $11\frac{1}{2}$"/29cm tall. The 'Weekenders' outfit was temporarily suspended. This Sindy came in a new box with a golden chain bracelet with a Sindy medallion attached to it and was in one of four new outfits:

'Ice Skating', a red circular skirt and tights/red and white knit jumper, hat and scarf with white skating boots.
'Miss Beautiful', a blue velvet dress with 'Sindy' sash.
'Beach Time Girl', a multi-striped top with yellow Bermuda shorts and sandals.
'Fashion Girl', a mauve checked mini dress with matching mauve shoes.

The 'Medallion Bracelet' had previously only been obtainable by joining the 'Sindy Club' at a price of three shillings. This bracelet was for the child to wear and to collect further charms to hook onto it. Sindy's outfits and separates remained virtually unchanged with just a few more additions (such as 'Town & Country', 'Career Girl' and 'Mini Gear'.

In the spring of 1968 Sindy was awarded the National Association of Toy Retailers' 'Toy of the Year' award at the London Trade Fair.

In 1969, Sindy was introduced wearing three new fashions: 'Evening Stroll', a navy reefer jacket with brass buttons and white slacks with ribbed top; 'Sunshine Girl', a pink floral print playtime pyjama suit; and 'Winter Warm', a fur-trimmed blue anorak and white trousers. For 1970, there were only two new outfits: 'Mini Skirt' and 'Outdoor Girl'.

Paul, too, was updated in 1966 to a slightly larger size of 12"/30cm, with a softer larger head and body with no markings at all. His clothes remained virtually the same with the addition of only a few more outfits: 'Camping', 'Tennis Party', 'Ship Ahoy', 'After Eight' and 'Brands Hatch', with separates such as jackets, blazer, flannels, raincoat, shirts, T-shirt, swim trunks and underwear.

From 1967 to 1969 a new French friend with a continental look was introduced for Sindy. She was called Mitzi and had blonde or red long, straight hair and large blue eyes. She came dressed in a blue roll-neck jumper and green wrap-over skirt, with green shoes and a small Eiffel

Tower charm in her box, which had a depiction of a French scene. The charm could be added to the Sindy 'Medallion Bracelet'. Mitzi was unmarked and at the same size as Sindy (12"/30cm) could wear all her clothes.

By 1967, the original-design Paul was discontinued in favour of a smart new Paul with rooted brown hair in a collar length long sideburns style; the face remained the same and he was $12\frac{1}{2}$"/31cm tall. He was marked 'Made in Hong Kong' on his back. He was, however, short-lived – by the end of that year Paul had been discontinued altogether, as were all his lovely Sixties fashions. A Scooter was introduced for Paul in 1967, but after his demise it became a Sindy accessory.

In 1965 'Mamselle Gear Get-Ups' had been introduced – 27 packs of fashion clothes for Sindy, and other teenage dolls, to compliment her already vast wardrobe. For 1967, 'Mamselle Gear Get-Ups' also included five fashions for Paul and five for Patch. The Paul outfits were made for just one year, while the Sindy and Patch outfits were discontinued in 1969. In 1966/67, 'Mamselle Dressing Up Clothes' were also introduced, this time for the child to dress up in. Authentic replicas of Sindy's outfits, they included: 'Leather Looker', 'Out and About', 'Weekenders', 'Bridesmaid' and 'Air Hostess', in sizes by age (3–6, 6–8 and 8–10). Patch followers were not forgotten either, with 'Dungarees' and 'Swan Lake' outfits in sizes 3–6 and 6–8 years.

Patch was given a new friend in 1968 called Poppet, with a similar size and face to Patch, but with an urchin hairstyle in three colours – blonde, auburn and brunette. She was boxed wearing a red jumper and tartan skirt and came with a 'Double Heart' charm to add to the Sindy 'Medallion Bracelet'. In 1970, Poppet was updated with a centre-parted, longer, straight black hairstyle with no fringe and came dressed in a striped coat-dress with matching hair band. She, too, was boxed with the 'Double Heart' charm for adding to the Sindy 'Medallion Bracelet'. This doll was discontinued in 1972; she was marked 'Hong Kong' on the back of her neck and the body was identical to Patch and marked '047001' across the shoulders.

Patch was updated with a new outfit, 'Blue Nightie' in 1970. Still issued with three shades of hair – blonde, auburn and brunette – in the straight fringed style, she was now taller than before, measuring 9"/23cm, and marked 'Made in England' on the back of her neck and '047001' across her shoulders. A 'Lucky Boot' charm came in her box from 1968, which could be added to the Sindy 'Medallion Bracelet'. By 1971, Patch's hairstyle had been changed slightly to a shorter, fuller more bouncy wavy style, but was still in the three shades. At the end of 1972, Patch was discontinued.

Springtime   Sweet Swimmer

Paul
the
well-dressed

Many more outfits had been introduced for Patch and included: 'Half Term', a tartan skirt and jumper with grey jacket; 'Hockey', a brown and yellow outfit with a hockey stick; 'Toboggan', a navy, hooded anorak and trousers with a toboggan; and 'Winter Time', a royal blue cord winter coat with white hat, scarf and muff. For more, see the complete list of Patch's outfits at the end of this chapter.

Sindy's new girlfriend was Vicki, introduced from 1968 to 1971. Slightly taller than the new, Basic Sindy at 12"/30cm tall, Vicki came with painted features including side-glancing blue eyes, but no lashes, a smiling mouth with a white line denoting teeth and masses of blonde short wavy hair. She was presented in a windowed box and dressed in a two-tier ribbon-trimmed sleeveless nylon lock-knit dress. She was unmarked on the back of her head and had the same five-jointed body as the early Sixties Sindy, which was also unmarked.

Several new Sindy's were introduced at the same time as Vicki, including: 'Walking Sindy' in 1969 with brunette or blonde side-parted hair with a 'flicked up' shoulder length style. Her legs enabled her to be walked along and she came dressed in a navy and red dot suit, available for one year only. For a further four years (1970–1973), this doll came dressed in a yellow polo-neck sweater and green and yellow checked mini skirt with yellow boots. A second outfit, a coat-dress, came in her box. She was $11\frac{1}{2}$"/29cm tall and marked 'Made in Hong Kong' on the back of her neck. The Sixties Sindys and fashions were phased out in 1970 to make way for an entirely new, mainly synthetic wardrobe of fashion clothes and a new Basic Sindy, introduced in 1971. This new doll was given centre-parted hair with shoulder-length curls and a blue hair band. She had painted blue eyes with eyelashes and retained the same Sindy face. She was available with blonde, auburn and brunette hair, measured $11\frac{1}{2}$"/29cm and was marked '033055X' on the back of her head, '033029' across the shoulders and '033030' on the small of the back. These new dolls were dressed in several styles, which included: 'Fun Furs', 'Miss Sindy', 'Fashion Girl', 'Day Girl' with 'Hot-pants' and 'Trendy Girl' in 1972. The dolls had six joints, including a twist waist. The fashions were made from synthetic fabrics in the latest colourful designs and included mini skirts, midi skirts, hot-pants, ponchos, catsuits, jumpsuits, smocks and fun-furs with names like 'Belle of the Ball', 'Top Pop Sindy, the all ActionGirl!', 'Super Sound Sindy' and 'Sindy Fun-Time'. The most exciting introduction, though, for 1971 was 'Lovely Lively Sindy', with centre-parted blonde, auburn or brunette hair and an alice band. She was advertised as 'Sindy has almost Come Alive', as she moved at the head, shoulders, elbows, waist, hips and knees. She had ten poseable joints with a slimmer twist and swivel waist and was the most poseable Sindy to date, with elbow joints, flexible knees and longer slimmer fingers. She came dressed in a jumpsuit with hair band and the Sindy Medallion Bracelet in her box. She measured $11\frac{1}{2}$"/29cm tall and was marked '033055X Made in Hong Kong'.

Seventies fashions had black heart-shaped tokens printed on the cellophane-fronted boxes and packages, and by collecting 24 heart tokens a child could send to the factory at Canterbury for a new doll called 'June'; introduced in 1972.

She was the same size as Patch, at 9"/23cm tall. She had short bouncy wavy hair in brown or fair (the child did not have the colour choices) and came wearing only white panties, although she could wear all the clothes designed for Patch. She had painted blue side-glancing eyes, five joints and fuller pink lips than Patch. She was marked '055001' on the back of her neck and '047001' across her back.

After six months (and as Patch was being discontinued at the end of 1972), June was upgraded to a Sindy-sized doll at $11\frac{1}{2}$"/29.5cm tall and could now wear all Sindy's lovely clothes. The second-issue June doll had forward-facing blue eyes, curly blonde hair, pale pink full lips and was marked '055014' on the back of her head and '033029' across her shoulders. The same 24 black printed hearts cut from the packs were needed to claim her. In 1973, June was upgraded again with side-glancing blue eyes, short fair straight hair and marked '055014' on the back of her neck and '033029' across her shoulders. As before, she came dressed in white panties and 24 black printed heart tokens were needed to claim her. This last model remained in production for one year.

As well as the many synthetic fabric fashions available for Sindy and friends in the early Seventies, Sindy had a white 'Bell Chime Piano' that played a tune, complete with a gilt-trimmed stool, an upholstered 'Settee, Easy Chair and Arm Chair' in a small cotton print, as well as a small cardboard two-roomed house with roof and chimneys. The back panel of the house pulls down to form the garden and give access to the two rooms. By 1974 it was updated to a flat-pack house with interchangeable rooms and no roof. Then, in the mid-Seventies, it was changed to a 'Scenesetter' rooms arrangement consisting of four printed board panels that slotted together to form four room scenes: kitchen, bathroom, sitting room and bedroom. 'Scenesetter' furniture was made to go with these rooms. As well as the 'Wardrobe and Bed', available since the Sixties, the early Seventies pieces were updated to include a new bed, wardrobe, white dressing table and stool, and a bedside table with battery-operated lamp. A white settee and chairs in P.V.C. with a white plastic gilt-decorated chest of drawers completed the scenes. Other new items for that year were: a red P.V.C. settee and chairs as an alternative to the white and a laminated dining table and four chairs, with a sideboard, also gilt-trimmed and full of crockery and cutlery with two golden candelabras. For the bathroom scene, the bath that filled with water and a 'working hairdryer' were new. The kitchen, too, had an updated sink unit and washday set consisting of a clothes horse and ironing board.

By the end of 1973, with Paul, Patch, Mitzi, Vicki, Betsy, Poppet and June all having been discontinued, Sindy was alone for her 10th Christmas. All the code numbers changed at this time, too, both on the dolls and the fashions and accessories. Pedigree was under new management. The one new doll in 1973 was 'Top Pop Sindy', dressed in a Daisy patterned co-ordinating blouse top and floral trousers. She was described as 'All Action Sindy – Raise her arm and Sindy will move her head, swing her hair and swivel her hips and legs. 'Sindy's Super Show', a clockwork turntable on which to display Sindy in her many beautiful new outfits was introduced in the early Seventies. The special outfits produced for this included 'Pop Show', 'Miss Sindy Beauty Queen', 'Elizabethan' and 'Startime'. At the same time, thirty heart tokens could be collected in exchange for a Sindy doll, now that June was no longer available. Other items were now available, too, for varying numbers of collected heart tokens.

From 1971, the Sindy Club was offering a Sindy Medallion Brooch instead of the Medallion Bracelet as a membership token.

In 1974, a new Basic Sindy with slimmer hands was introduced, marked '033055X' on the back of the head and measuring 11"/28cm tall. In the same year, Lovely Lively Sindy was replaced by 'Active Sindy' – the most poseable doll ever, with fifteen joints. Active Sindy was petite, being only 11"/28cm tall. She was marked 'Sindy 033055X' on the back of her head and 'Hong Kong' on the small of her back. She came dressed in a white leotard, tights and ballet shoes with a lilac tutu. Her face and hairstyle were similar to the 1971 Basic Sindy, but perhaps a little daintier, and her hair was tied back with a ribbon. She, too, was available with blonde, auburn and brunette hair. After a year the lilac tutu was replaced with a pink tutu and she was called 'Ballerina Sindy'. The same doll was available dressed in an ice-skating outfit, with skating boots and was called 'Super Star Sindy'.

In 1977, the year of the Queen's Silver Jubilee, a 'Royal Occasion Sindy' was introduced to mark the occasion. Available for one year only, she was a basic doll with the new-style slimmer hands and flexible legs and came wearing a cream lace-trimmed long gown and matching picture hat with parasol. She had dark blonde centre-parted hair and was marked '033055X' on the back of her head. She was 11"/28cm tall.

In 1978, a black friend was produced called Gayle. This doll looked the same as Active Sindy, but she had glossy, black centre-parted hair and brown painted side-glancing eyes. She had the same body as the Active Sindy and came dressed in a red floral pinafore dress and white blouse. Together with a blonde Active Sindy, she was the first of the collection to be distributed in the U.S.A. (by Marx Toys). Both dolls were marked '2 GEN 033055X' on

the back of the head and 'Made in Hong Kong' on the small of their backs. They measured 11"/28cm tall and one other outfit was issued as an alternative. 'Sweet Dreams Sindy' was the new doll for 1979. She, too, measured 11"/28cm tall and had sleeping eyes with lashes. The eyes were the painted, sleeping type and this doll was available only with blonde or brunette rooted hair. She came dressed in her blue nightwear and slippers and was marked '033390' on the back of her head. Later models were dressed in a tiny floral negligee and an apricot nightie with brown lace trim. By the late Seventies the Sindy 'Medallion Bracelet' and charms had been discontinued from all the boxes and Sindy hearts with a black S in the centre were being cut out and saved from the packaging to be exchanged for gifts that were being updated all the time.

Also introduced in the mid- to late-Seventies were 'Sindy Styling Heads', available in three different sizes – 7"/18cm, then 12"/30cm and $3\frac{1}{2}$"/9cm – and with blonde or brunette rooted hair. Each came with a brush, comb, curlers, grips and various accessories and a style guide.

A lovely new self-assembly 'Town House' for Sindy heralded the start of the Eighties. Made from decorated board and plastic and standing 4'3" (130cm) high by 12"/30cm deep, it had three floors, with a lift and a small spiral staircase to the rooftop patio area. The floors accommodated a kitchen, bathroom, bedroom and living room. The furniture of the early Seventies was now updated again to go with the super new house. There was a new yellow bathroom suite with brown towels and accessories, Eastham yellow kitchen units, a split-level cooker and a washing machine. These units resembled the real kitchen units seen in many British homes of the Seventies. For Sindy's dining room there was a 'glass' fronted dresser to display china and a white dining table and chairs. For her lounge a 'buttoned' rounded style settee and easy chairs were available in pale-yellow moulded P.V.C. with loose covers and cotton curtains to match. There were other items too, such as a coffee table, lamp and rocking chair. A hostess trolley with plastic food ensured that Sindy did not go hungry. A writing desk and stool came with tiny notepaper and pencils. For outside, there was a swimming pool that filled with water and a country garden with a lean-to greenhouse, rockery and flower pots. Other outdoor items available included a horse and horsebox, camper, beach buggy and a tent.

In case you wanted to take Sindy with you wherever you went, the bright pink 'Carry-me-Case' from 1967/68 was re-introduced, but now with a round handle instead of the original square one. There was room enough in the case to hold a Sindy doll and many items of her wardrobe on little hangers. There was also a 'Hotel Room', which folded into a suitcase with room enough for a fold-down bed, a Sindy doll and her clothes.

The list of furniture, vehicles and accessories was growing all the time. Sindy was enjoying boom years and the factory at Canterbury was working in shifts round the clock to keep up production of all items, and packaging and assembling nearly 4,000 Sindy dolls a day. (The head and Sindy clothing was made in their factory in Hong Kong.) Sindy was being exported to 75 countries.

Through the early Seventies, the outfits were still code numbered and 'named', but the labels were changed to either printed cotton with 'Genuine Sindy Made in Hong Kong' on the more expensive ones or just a paper label with 'Made in Hong Kong' on the pocket-money fashions. Towards the end of the Seventies and into the early Eighties, many garments were unmarked, or the more expensive outfits were marked with just a printed 'Sindy' label. Once the unmarked garments had lost their packaging they were difficult to identify and attribute to Sindy. Not all the items of clothing were pictured in the catalogues as at this time and many hundreds of different outfits were being made, some of them for special orders or export only.

The start of the Eighties also saw many changes and new additions to the Sindy range of products. The packaging with the black heart was replaced with a bright pink heart and tiny white heart tokens with a bright pink 'S' on them were introduced for children to collect in exchange for gifts. On the celebration of Sindy's 18th birthday, retailers were presented with a special Sindy Doll as a gift for their custom. New Sindy models for the early Eighties included: 'Styling Sindy', 'Party Time Sindy', 'Quick Change Sindy', 'Regency Sindy' and 'Masquerade Sindy' (with a mass of tiny curls in each of the three colours). By the mid Eighties, these were joined by 'Space Fantasy Sindy' with lovely pink hair and silver space costume, and 'Shaping Up Sindy' with two long blonde plaits and leotard outfit. The 1980s fashions included 'Nostalgia', 'Classics', 'Boutique', 'Casual', 'Elegance' and 'Designer Fashions'.

By 1986 Pedigree was finding it hard to cope with competition and experienced a drop in sales as children drifted away in their thousands from traditional toys towards videogames. A new stylish Sindy was commissioned from Media Designers to attract children back to dolls and toys. The new Sindys, with a new face, were: 'Fun Time Sindy', 'Disco Magic Sindy' (with two tone auburn and pink hair), 'Starlight Sindy', 'Silver Skater Sindy', 'Magic Moments Sindy' (with changing hair colours), 'Sindy Goes to Dallas' (after the glitzy TV programme), 'Jazzdance Sindy', 'Snow Princess Sindy', 'Romance and Roses Sindy', 'Ballerina Sindy' and 'My First Sindy' (with blonde, auburn or brunette hair and at a more pocket-money price). All were beautifully window boxed in lavish costumes.

New friends, also introduced in 1986, were Mark and Marie, with two different outfits each. 'Fashion-Loving Mark' had blue-and-white casual clothes and 'Jazzdance Mark' matched Jazzdance Sindy in pink-and-green Lycra. Marie's two outfits were an emerald-green and black two-piece suit and a blue and white striped two-piece suit. Both outfits and dolls were very eye-catching, as Marie had shoulder-length rooted red hair, while Mark had moulded brown hair. Both were robust looking dolls of 12"/30cm tall. Marie was marked 'Marie' on the back of the neck and Mark was just marked 'Pedigree Dolls & Toys' across his back.

Many new separate outfits were introduced for these new dolls, including 'Designer Classics' and 'Designer Emanuel' (the designers of Lady Diana Spencer's wedding dress). There were four gorgeous ensembles in bright vivid red, orange, pink and yellow. Sindy had never been more eye-catching! One of the last boxed sets from Pedigree was 'Royal Wedding Mark and Marie', who resembled HRH Prince Andrew and Miss Sarah Ferguson on their wedding day.

At the end of 1986 Sindy and Friends were sold to Hasbro Inc, the American toy giant, and Sindy was re-issued by them for 1987 with another different face as 'City Girl Sindy' and with a reinvented boyfriend, Paul. These dolls were produced into the Nineties, when Sindy was again sold, this time to Vivid Imaginations. Sindy is quite a different and more mature young woman today than the sweet English teenage doll that began it all in September 1963.

The first two original Sindy Booklets 1963 and 1964 which detail the first classic separately packed fashions for Sindy. (See list at end of this chapter.)

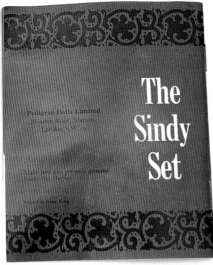

Clockwise from top left:

Tammy 1962
Ideal Corp. U.S.A.
12"/30.5cm
© *Ideal Toy Corp*
Blonde Tammy wears her original blue/white jumpsuit and white tie-up shoes. She has rooted hair and painted features with right side glancing eyes.

Sindy
Pedigree Dolls & Toys
12"/30.5cm
Made in England
September 1963
Brunette original Sindy wears 'Weekenders' red/blue/white striped cotton knit top and blue jeans with yellow stitching, white tie-up shoes and an Alice band in her rooted hair. She has painted features with right side glancing eyes.

Pages from the early 60s Sindy set fashion booklet showing some of the classic styles available for Sindy during the sixties.

Sindy
Pedigree Dolls & Toys
11¼"/28.5cm
'Made in England' on small of back
1965
Three Sindy dolls, brunette, blonde, auburn dressed in their original 'Weekenders' outfits which were available from 1963 to 1967, before appearing again in 1971 on a Basic Sindy.

139

Sindy
Pedigree
11¼"/28.5cm
Made in England on small of back
1965
Three 2nd issue Sindy dolls, left to right:
Brunette wearing 'Centre Court' tennis dress
Blonde wearing 'Leather Looker' red flared hipster
Auburn wearing 'Emergency Ward' student Nurse.

Sindy
Pedigree
12"/30.5cm
Made in England on back of neck
1963
Three 1963 Sindys left to right:
Brunette wearing 'Out & About'
Blonde 'Country Walk' complete with Poodle Dog, Ringo.
Auburn doll wearing 'Springtime' blouse and 'Summer Walks' skirt.
These outfits were featured on the television campaign launching Sindy in
September 1963.

Sindy
Pedigree
11½"/29cm / 12"/30.5cm
Made in Hong Kong / Made in England
1968 / 1963
From left to right:
A 1968 Sindy with pale blonde side parted hair wears 'Trim Trouser Suit'
and 'Windy Days' royal blue tam o' shanter, scarf and muff. 1963 Auburn
Sindy wears 'Bridesmaid' yellow chiffon dress; 1963 brunette Sindy wears
'Cape'.

Sindy
Pedigree
11½"/29cm / 12"/30.5cm
Made in Hong Kong / Made in England
1968 / 1963
From left to right:
1968 Sindy wears 'Bridesmaid' white lawn and broderies anglais dress.
Brunette 1963 Sindy wears 'Out & About'. Blonde 1963 Sindy wears
'Summery Days'.

Sindy
Pedigree
11½"/29cm
Made in Hong Kong
1968
Three 1968 Sindys from left to right: wearing 'Lunch Date', 'Happy Traveller' and 'Smock Dress'.

Sindy
Pedigree
11½"/29cm
Made in Hong Kong
These three blonde 1968 Sindys are wearing, from left to right 'Pony Club', 'Shopping in the Rain' and 'Air Hostess'.

Sindy / Mitzi / Vicki / June
Pedigree
11½"/29cm / 12"/30.5cm / 12"/30.5cm / 11¾"/30cm
Made in Hong Kong / no markings / no markings / 0055014 003029
Dates: 1968/71 / 1967/69 / 1968/71 1973
Sindy's three friends could all wear Sindy's clothes, left to right:
Sindy in 'Happy Traveller' 1965
Mitzi in 'Trouser Suit' 1966 & 'Windy Day' 1963
Vicki in 'Fur Fashion' 1967
June (3rd issue) in 'Duffle Coat' 1963.

Mitzi / Vicki / June (2) / June (3)
Pedigree Dolls & Toys
12"/30.5cm / 12"/30.5cm / 11¾"/30cm / 11¾"/30cm
Dates: 1967/69 / 1968/71 / 1972 / 1973
Mitzi in 'Trouser Suit' 1966 & 'Windy Day' 1963
Vicki in 'Fur Fashion' 1967
June (2) in 'Shopping in the Rain' 1963
June (3) in 'Cosy Coat' 1972.

Paul/Sindy/Patch
Pedigree
11¾"/30cm / 11¼"/28.5cm / 8½"/22cm
Made in Hong Kong / Made in England / Made in Hong Kong
1965 / 1965 / 1965
1965 moulded hair Paul wearing 'Casuals'
1965 Sindy wearing 'Weekenders'
1965 Patch wearing 'Dungarees'
*Pictured with Sindy's red plastic two seater MGB Sports Car with chrome bumpers,
hub caps and headlamps. Made from 1964 to 1969.*

Sindy/Paul
Pedigree
11¼"/28.5cm / 11¼"/28.5cm
Made in England / Made in Hong Kong
1965 / 1965
*1965 Sindy wears 'Weekenders' and 1965 Paul wears
'Casuals'. These two outfits were made to compliment one
another as were Country Walk/Motorway Man; Pony
Club/Time Off; Lunch Date/London Look; Emergency
Ward/Medical Student; Winter Holiday/Winter Sports;
Bowling/Soccer etc.*

Paul
Pedigree
12"/30.5cm / 11¾"/30cm
no markings / Made in Hong Kong
1966 / 1965
From left to right:
A 1966 Paul in his Y fronts.
A 1965 Paul wearing part of 'And So to Bed'.
A 1965 Paul in 'Swimming Trunks'.

Paul
Pedigree
12"/30.5cm / 11¾"/30cm
no markings / Made in Hong Kong
1966 / 1965
From left to right:
A 1966 Paul in 'Time Off'.
A 1965 version in 'Casuals'.
A 1966 Paul wearing 'Motorway Man'.

Paul
Pedigree
12¼"/31cm / 11¾"/30cm
Made in Hong Kong
Dates: 1967 / 1965
From left to right:
A rooted brown haired Paul
available only in 1967 and
wearing 'Blazer and Casuals'.
Two 1965 Pauls, wearing
'London Look' and 'Casual
Jacket' and jeans.

Springtime

A pretty, practical blouse that will team up with other skirts or slacks. Made in crisp, gay printed cotton, it has long push-up sleeves, frilled at the waist, and buttons at the back. Available in assorted colours. 12S19
Complete with hanger **4 6d**

Sweet Swimmer

In the water and out of Sindy is the sweetest swimmer in her demure swim-suit with the new, covered-up look. Sindy's swimsuit is in royal blue jersey to match her eyes and a white neckline border sets off her tan. Sandals complete the outfit. 12S60
Complete with hanger **5 11d**

Sindy's Car

Sindy's the envy of all her friends because she's got every grown-up girl's dream: a red two-seater sportscar! It's perfect in every detail with chrome fenders, hubcaps and headlamps. Finished dashboard and sleek wide windscreen. Radio aerial has Sindy banner to flutter in the breeze. 12SA1
29 11d

Sindy's Wardrobe

Sindy keeps her outfits and accessories in her own modern, design graphic doors spacious wardrobe. Inside left doors full length mirror and shoe racks. On the reverse, top shelf she stores hats and boxes and keeps her lingerie in the special built-in cabinet. 12SA2
Complete with hanger **25 6d**

Paul the well-dressed young man

Who's the luckiest girl in town? Sindy! Because she now has a super boyfriend, Paul. He's got a smart collection of clothes – the type of wardrobe every girl would like her boyfriend to wear, all tailormade with handsome detail.

Paul is keen on music and dancing and he and Sindy go to jazz clubs and dances.

Like Sindy, he likes a good time and has clothes are designed for a free-wheeling life. His wardrobe is shown on the following pages.

Paul in Casuals

At weekends, and casual parties, Paul wears slim-line 14-inch bottom blue jean hipsters with yellow stitching. Matched with a bulky knit green or red pull-over with polo-neck and white sneakers. Outfit designed to go with Sindy's 'Weekenders'. Paul has bendable limbs. 13MPS
Doll complete in casuals with stand and style book **24 11d**

Seaside

Paul wears a Continental-type slash-necked jacket and matched shorts in red denim for lounging on the beach. This outfit comes with sandals, sunglasses, towel and water-skis. For seaside snap-taking Paul has a camera with strap. 13M02
Complete with style book **17/6d**

Motorway Man

For motoring around town or taking country walks with Sindy, Paul chooses a mottled brown left tie-coat with a brown houndstooth pullover + black polo-necked pullover. Paul's brown/black checked trousers match Sindy's 'Country Walk' skirt. Flask and mug complete Paul's outfit. 13M04
Complete with style book **25 11d**

London Look

When Paul takes Sindy to a show he wears his elegant sand-coloured slim-line blue wool suit with four-button jacket and fish-tail back. The blue lines shirt has a high collar and a blue knit tie. Paul wears a matching blue handkerchief in his breast pocket and black Chelsea boots. 13M03
Complete with style book **22 11d**

And so to bed

When it's time to retire Paul dons his blue and white striped pyjamas and dresses. He's got a matching three-quarter length dressing gown with tie belt to match, too. All an exclusive no-collar style with an Oriental touch. Electric razor, slippers and sponge bag with flannel and soap, comb and brush, toothbrush and paste. 13M01
Complete with style book **19 11d**

Time Off

For casual dates at coffee bars with Sindy, Paul wears his fuller-lined jacket made of brown suedette with front pockets, grey and white checked poplin shirt and matching duffle bag and yellow string tie. The trousers are fawn slim-cut trilby over brown Chelsea boots. With Pop Group Poster. 13M05
Complete with style book **25 11d**

Tee-shirt

Paul sports the wide-necking tee-shirt of white cotton knit of hole-dots and summer uses aside. It's got Paul's initial in red. 13M51
Complete with hanger **5 11d**

Casual Jacket

Every well-dressed man needs a casual jacket. Paul's is a mottled blue and black collarless style made with wool and stretch fabric. It's cut straight for free and easy movement and looks. Black, shiny buttons. 13M53
Complete with hanger **9 6d**

Swimming Trunks

On the beach Paul looks a knockout in his blue and black bikini-striped swimsuit. It's made of closely-woven stretch fabric for fit and comfort. 13M52
Complete with hanger **3 6d**

Sindy Cut-out and Keep Busy Books

Sindy Cut-out Books

Follow Sindy's gay adventures in town and country. Each book contains a cut-out of Sindy and authentic cardboard versions of her clothes.
Book complete with cut-outs **2 6d**

Sindy Keep Busy Books

Spend many happy hours with Sindy Keep Busy Books. Each book contains puzzles, new games and Sindy pictures and stories to colour.
Book complete with 80 pages **2 6d**

SINDY wallpaper

Now! Your room can be a Sindy room

SINDY wallpaper

Wake up with Sindy, spend the day with Sindy, say goodnight with Sindy. Have a Sindy wallpaper!

Sindy (and Paul and Patch) will come to life in your room with the new Sindy Wallpaper, a really up-to-the-minute, fashionable wallpaper with lovely colours.

Redecorate with Sindy Wallpaper, made specially for you by I.C.I., and sold at the special price of only 9s. 8d. per roll (plus 6d. Purchase Tax).

Ask for Sindy Wallpaper at your local wallpaper shop. (Available only in the U.K.)

Some Paul fashions from the sixties. The illustration also shows Sindy Wallpaper depicting the early sixties Sindy Dolls and fashions.

Left:
The first Sindy Set fashion booklet shows a few fashion clothes available for Paul through the sixties.

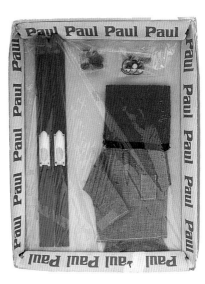

'Seaside' boxed outfit for Paul contains red
denim two-piece with sandals, sunglasses,
camera, water skis and towel.

'Soccer' boxed outfit for Paul contains yellow and blue shirt, shorts
and socks with fooball boots, shin pad and ball.

'Medical Student' boxed outfit for Paul contains white cotton suit
with germ mask, stethoscope, shoes and skeleton.

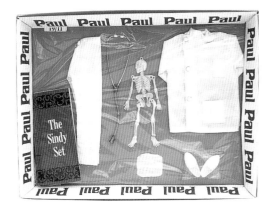

Opposite page: from left to right:
Paul
Pedigree
11¾"/30cm / 12"/30.5cm / 12½"/31cm
Made in Hong Kong / No markings / Made in Hong Kong
1965 / 1966 / 1967
*Original moulded hair Paul and box wearing 'Casuals' 2nd Issue moulded
hair Paul. This updated version of Paul with rooted brown hair was made for
one year only. He had painted brown eyes and eyebrows, pink lips and was
boxed dressed in his 'Casuals' outfit.*

'Sailing' a boxed outfit for Sindy containing oilskin jacket,
trousers and sou'wester with duffle bag and lifebelt.

Sindy
Pedigree
$11\frac{1}{4}$"/28.5cm $11\frac{1}{2}$"/29cm
Made in England / Made in Hong Kong
1965 1968

Standing 1965 Sindy wears 'Sleepy Time' baby doll nightie and 'Cosy Nights' dressing gown. Seated on Sindy's Hollywood style bed is a 1968 auburn side parting Sindy wearing 'Undie World'. On the chair, a brunette 1965 Sindy wearing 'Frosty Nights'.

Sindy's Medallion Bracelet and Charms. Each Sindy doll sold after 1968 had the Medallion Bracelet in the box and each of Sindy's friends, (with the exception of the Junes) had a charm in their box that the child could add to the bracelet.

A selection of Sindy fashion booklets from 1964 to 1986, were to be found in the boxes of Sindy clothes and accessories.

Two early sixties boxed jigsaws and two Annuals depicting the Sindy Set. Cut-out Paper Doll books and Colouring and Puzzle books were also available depicting the Sindy Set.

Gear Get Ups Leaflet
The Pedigree Mamselle leaflet depicting 'Sunday Best', 'Gad-Abouts' and 'Fan Club' for Sindy and 12" teen dolls.

Clockwise from right:

Patch
Pedigree
8½"/22cm
Made in Hong Kong
1965
Three 1965 Patch dolls showing the different hair colours: auburn, blonde, and brunette.
All are wearing their original 'Dungarees' outfits.

Patch
Pedigree
8½"/22cm
Made in Hong Kong
1965
Three Patch dolls with straight fringed hair
wearing from left to right: 'Swan Lake',
'Brownie' – 1st Merton Pack, and 'Sou'wester'.
This outfit was also available in yellow with black Wellingtons.

Patch
Pedigree
9"/23cm
Made in England 047001
1971
From left to right:
The brunette wears 'Pinafore & Blouse', the blonde
'Home for the Day' check pinafore and 'Easylife' black jumper and tights,
while the auburn wears 'Smocked Dress'.

Patch
Pedigree
9"/23cm
Made in England 047001
1971
By the early seventies Patch had been updated with a new curly hairstyle still available in blonde, auburn and brunette.
From left to right:
'Birthday Party'
'Schooldays' and
'Red Riding Hood'.

Patch

Pedigree
8 ½"/22cm
Made in Hong Kong
1965
A blonde Patch and box wearing her original 'Dungarees' outfit.

The 'Half Term' boxed outfit for Patch included a tartan skirt, red jumper and grey jacket, with socks, shoes and white kitten.

Poppet

Pedigree
9"/23cm
Hong Kong & 047001
1968/70
Poppet with her urchin cut hairstyle and Patch's red jumper and tartan skirt from 'Half Term' 1966.

'Summer Special' and 'Easter Parade' mint in pack outfits for Patch.

'Toboggan' and 'Hockey' mint in pack outfits for Patch.

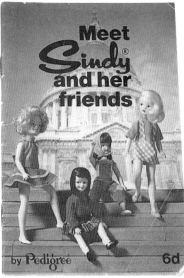

Sindy's 1968 and 1969 Booklets depicting new dolls, outfits and accessories, plus Sindy's friends.

A page from Sindy's 1968 Booklet depicting Patch, Poppet and Betsy with their fashions and accessories.

A page from Sindy's 1969 Booklet depicting Mitzi and Vicki and their golden charms for attaching to the Sindy Medallion Bracelet.

Clockwise, from above:

June
Pedigree
9"/23cm / 11$\frac{3}{4}$"/30cm / 11$\frac{3}{4}$"/30cm
055001 and 047002 / 055014 and 033029 / 055014 and 033029
1972 / 1972 / 1973
From left to right:
The three issues of June comprise a Patch sized doll, Issue 2 and Issue 3.
All are pictured as supplied wearing nylon panties for dressing in either Patch or Sindy Fashions.

Basic Sindy
Pedigree
11$\frac{1}{2}$"/29cm
033055X head. 033029 across shoulders. 033030 across small of back.
1971
Three Basic Sindys: a brunette wearing 'Look Warm', the blonde wearing 'Skater' and an auburn wearing a 'Mod Suit'.

Basic Sindy
Pedigree
11$\frac{1}{2}$"/29cm
033055X head. 033029 across shoulders. 033030 across small of back.
1971
Three blonde Basic Sindys, from left to right, wearing 'Springtime', 'Cosy Coat' and 'Funtime'.

Lovely Lively Sindy
Pedigree
11$\frac{1}{2}$"/29cm
033055X Made in Hong Kong
1971
Three Lovely Lively Sindys with blonde, auburn and brunette rooted soft hair. Each has a slimmer body with ten poseable joints which included swivel waist and elbows, and long separate fingers.

A page of beautiful fashions from the 1972 Catalogue. At left: 'Miss Beautiful'
Top left to right: 'Queen of the Ball', 'Blazer Way', Skater, 'Red Hot Dress and
Coat', 'College Girl', 'Disco Party', and 'Shiny Shopper'.
Bottom left to right: 'Cosy Coat', 'Pinny Party', 'Bridesmaid', 'Zinga Ding',
'Theatre Time', 'Checker Decker' and 'Summer Party'.

Sindy's red Beach Buggy with opening
bonnet and folding windscreen. Basic
Sindy wears 'New Dungarees' from the
1973 catalogue.

This early seventies Sindy catalogue Basic Sindys modelling shows two from left
to right: 'Funtime' and 'Apple', and two Lovely Lively Sindys modelling 'Classic
Dress' and 'Flared Trousers'.

Sindy's Saturday Pocket-money Fashions
Basic Sindy wears low-priced separates
from the 1973 Catalogue.

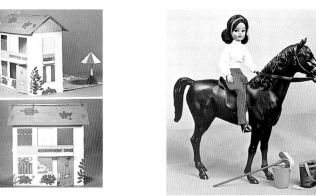

A strong card two-roomed Sindy
House with roof, chimneys and a
back panel that dropped down to
give access to the two rooms and
form a garden area. 1970s.

Basic Sindy on 'Peanuts' with
accessories and wearing 'Jodpurs with
hat' from the 1973 catalogue.

Sindy's Super Show was
a clockwork turntable for
displaying Sindy in her
outfits specially-produced
outfits including 'Ballet',
'Pop Show', 'Beauty
Queen', 'Elizabethan'
and 'Startime'. From
the 1972 Catalogue.

Left, from top to bottom:

Sindy's 1970 dining table and chairs in white plastic with 'Formica' top and red velvet chair seats, together with sideboard, candlesticks, cutlery, crockery, glasswear and silver tea set.
Pictured at the 'Dinner Party' are left to right:
Lovely Lively Sindy 1971 wearing 'Party Time' 1972,
Basic 1971 Sindy wearing 'Midi Look' 1972,
Lovely Lively Sindy 1971 wearing 'Day Girl' 1971,
Basic Sindy 1971 wearing 'Summer Party' 1972.

Sindy's 1971 white lounge settee and armchairs with 1968 chest of drawers.
From left to right:
Lovely Lively Sindy 1971 wearing 'Floral Suit' 1972,
Basic Sindy 1971 wearing 'Cat Suit' 1970,
Basic Sindy 1971 wearing 'Trendy Girl' 1972,
Basic Sindy 1971 wearing 'New Dungarees' 1972.

Sindy's wardrobe available in the early 60s had legs until it was updated in 1967 in the version shown, together with Sindy's 'Gown Rail' and an assortment of fashions from the early seventies. Beside it stands Basic Sindy 1971 wearing 'Fun Furs'.

Sindy's 'Scenesetter' Home in the mid seventies consisted of four printed board panels that slotted together to form four room scenes: kitchen/bathroom /sitting room/bedroom.

1967 Sindy's Bath. Working model complete with accessories. A pink hairdryer, also a working model, was issued at the same time.

Sindy's bedroom furniture from the 'Scenesetter' range showing the new white bed, dressing table and stool, rocking chair, wardrobe, bedside table, lamp, and breakfast tray with crockery. Circa 1976.

Sindy's new lounge furniture from the 'Scenesetter' range. The style was the same white settee and armchairs shown opposite. Mid seventies.

Sindy's kitchen furniture from the 'Scenesetter' range showing the lovely 'Eastham' yellow kitchen units and 'Washday Accessories'.

Sindy's bathroom furniture from the 'Scenesetter' range.

Sweet Dreams Sindy
Pedigree
11"/28cm
033390 on the back of the neck
1979

This illustration shows the three versions of
Sweet Dreams Sindy, the only Sindy made
with painted 'sleeping' eyes and eyelashes. On
the right, is the original Sweet Dreams dressed
in a blue nylon and lace nightgown from 1979.
On the left, she wears a tiny floral print cotton
nightdress and negligee set from in 1980 and
in the centre a brown floral nightdress with
brown lace trim from the early eighties. Many
other nightwear outfits were issued for these
dolls including pyjamas, nightshirts and nightie
and negligee sets in various different fabrics
through the early eighties.

Sindy's suitcase 'Hotel Room'
This item, which included a bed, shower, shelves and mirror and hanging space for clothes, was introduced in 1979. The whole thing folded into a 'Carry Case' for a Sindy doll and her clothes.

Gayle and Sindy
Marx Toys under licence from Pedigree
11"/28cm
2 GEN1977 033055X
Made in Hong Kong
1978
Gayle was a black Active Sindy lookalike and together with a blonde Active Sindy, they were the first Sindy dolls available in the U.S.A. distributed by Marx under licence from Pedigree. They were only available from a few outlets in the States. Pictured in the scene is the export version of the Sindy table and chairs, with maroon seats whereas in Britain they were green.

Walking Sindy

12WS1 Walking Sindy – Just look at 'Walking Sindy' – hold her waist and make her walk along . . . She has a yellow polo neck sweater and matching green and yellow check mini skirt and boots, there's a coat dress too . . . Sindy always likes to keep in fashion! ♡♡

Walking Sindy
Pedigree
11½"/29cm
Made in Hong Kong
1969 to 1973
Walking Sindy was introduced with two outfits – the check mini skirt and jumper pictured here from the 1970 catalogue and a floral coat dress with chain belt. In 1969 she was issued wearing a suit in navy with red dots for one year only.

June
Pedigree
11¾"/30cm
055014 neck. 033029 across shoulders
1973
Sindy's friend June was not available in the toy stores but only by collecting heart tokens from the packs and redeeming 24 token by sending to the factory. By 1974 a Sindy Doll was offered for 30 tokens.

This leaflet accompanied the Sindy dolls and accessories that were sold in the United States.

Space Fantasy Masquerade Side-parting
Pedigree
Sizes: 11"/28cm
Sindy 033055X
Dates: 1985 / 1983 / 1979
Pink haired 'Space Fantasy' Sindy on the left wears a pink satin dress from the 'Reflection' fashions. Brunette 'Masquerade' Sindy has an abundance on tiny curls, while a late seventies auburn side parting Sindy wears a mid blue evening gown.

Active Sindy
Pedigree
11"/28cm
Sindy 033055X Hong Kong
1974
These three Sindy's are the daintiest of all the versions and were available with blonde, auburn or brunette rooted centre-parted hair tied back in a little curly bun. They had fifteen poseable joints and are illustrated in their original ballet outfits of white leotard, tights and ballet shoes with Lilac tutu.

Sindy
Pedigree
11"/28cm
033055X on the back of the head
1974 / 1977 / 1975
On the left are two Basic Sindys 1974 with the newer slimmer hands and short centre-parted rooted hair. They were both boxed as 'Funtime' Sindys. Centre right is 'Royal Occasion Sindy' 1977 dressed for Ascot in a long cream lace trimmed gown with picture hat and parasol. This doll was issued for H.M. Queen Elizabeth's Silver Jubilee, for one year only. On the right: 'Active Sindy' 1975 now dressed in a white or pink tutu instead of the lilac one.

Styling Sindy
Sindy Pop Singer
Shaping Up Sindy
Pedigree
11"/28cm
Sindy 033055X
Dates: 1980 / 1982 / 1985
Over the years Sindy has had a variety of different hairstyles.
Pictured here on the left: waist length hair 'Styling Sindy' wearing 'Modern Miss'.
Centre: short bubble cut hair on 'Sindy Pop Singer' wearing her original smock.
On the right: two plaits 'Shaping Up' Sindy wearing a ballet tutu.

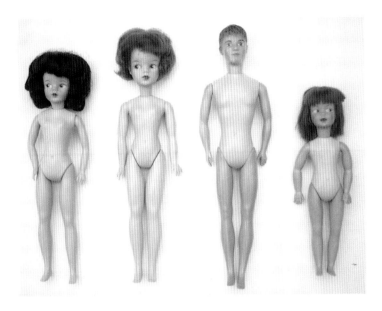

From left to right: 1965 Sindy with five joints and wired slightly poseable limbs.
11¾″/28.5cm, unmarked.
1963 Sindy with hollow softer bendable arms, non-posing legs, five joints,
12″/30.5cm, marked Made in England on the back of her neck.
1965 Paul with wired slightly poseable limbs and five joints.
11¾″/30cm, marked Made in Hong Kong.
1965 Patch with wired slightly poseable limbs and five joints.
8½″/22cm, marked Made in Hong Kong.

From left to right:
1968 side parting Sindy with wired poseable limbs and six joints,
including twist waist. 11½″/29cm, marked Made in Hong Kong.
This is the most flexible of all the early Sindys and the first to be
given eye lashes.
1967 Rooted Hair Paul with wire slightly poseable limbs and five
joints. 12¼″/31cm, marked Made in Hong Kong. This doll was only
issued in 1967.
1971 Patch with wired slightly poseable limbs and five joints.
9″/23cm, marked Made in England 047001.

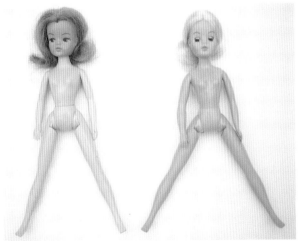

Left to right: 1971 Basic Sindy with eyelashes, hollow limbs and six joints
including a twist waist. 11½″/29cm, marked 033055X on head, 033029 on
shoulder, 033030 on small of back.
1971 Lovely Lively Sindy with eye lashes, ten joints and flexible knees with
long slim fingers, 11½″/29cm, marked 033055X Made in Hong Kong.
1974 Active Sindy with eye lashes and fifteen poseable joints (some flexible),
making her the most poseable Sindy. 11″/28cm, marked Sindy 033055X
Hong Kong.

Left: 1974 Basic Sindy with eyelashes, eight poseable joints and new
slimmer fingers. 11″/28cm, marked 033055X on back of head.
Right: 1979 Sweet Dreams Sindy with sleeping eyes and eyelashes.
She had the basic Sindy body with eight poseable joints and slimmer
fingers. 11″/28cm, marked 033390 on the back of the head.

Sindy Styling Heads
Pedigree
3 sizes: 12"/31cm; 7"/18cm; 3½"/9cm (not shown)
Pedigree
Late seventies

On the left, a large styling head with long fringed, rooted blonde hair. On the right, a brunette centre parted hairstyle in a medium size. A small styling head the same size as those on the dolls was also available, issued with 'Quick Change Sindy' in the early eighties. All the heads came with brush, comb, curlers, grips and accessories for hours of play. They were all available in blonde or brunette haircolours.

Three new Basic Sindys for 1986. These dolls were made for less than a year. 11½"/29cm, marked Sindy on the back of the neck, with five joints and straight legs. A more poseable version with twist waist and flexible legs was also made during 1986.

These two posters from the early eighties shows the extent and amazing quantity of items now being made for Sindy from fashion clothes, accessories, and furniture, to vehicles and houses which were updated several times during the early to mid eighties.

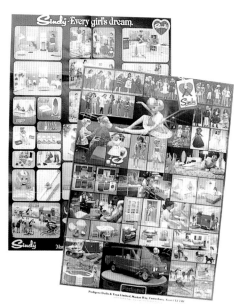

This lovely home was introduced for Sindy in 1980 and comprised three floors and rooftope patio standing over four feet tall. Optional extras included: balcony, internal doors, windows, lighting, a fireplace, soft furnishings and extra room Extension packs i.e. Bedroom and Stable/Garage. Any number could be added to enlarge the existing house, as seen in the illustration.

Marie and Mark were two new friends for Sindy introduced in 1986 and also made for less than a year. Marie had six joints including twist waist, she was 12"/30cm tall and marked Marie on the back of the neck. Mark had five movable joints, was 12"/30.5cm tall and marked Pedigree Dolls and Toys across his back. Both are wearing their original outfits. Two other different outfits were also issued, plus a Mark and Marie 'Royal Wedding' Gift Set in 1986.

In mid-1973, with the company under new management, all the original code numbers were changed.
Any earlier items that were retained were renumbered and a completely new numbering system was introduced,
which is more difficult to follow as the numbers did not run consecutively.

12GSS	Sindy Doll in 'Weekenders' outfit 1963/64 and updated for 1965/67.	
	(The 'Weekenders outfit was issued on all dressed Sindy dolls from 1963 to 1967,	
	then re-issued for one year on Basic Sindy in 1971.)	
12GSO	Sindy doll, naked	1964.
13MPS	Paul Doll in 'Casuals'	1965 to 1966.
9GPS	Patch Doll in 'Dungarees'	1965 to 1966.
13MPS	Paul Doll with rooted hair in 'Casuals'	1967 only.
6GBS	Betsy Doll in 'Red cord dress' with stars and stripes badge	1967 to 1969.
12GMH	Mitzi Doll in 'Blue jumper, green skirt and shoes' .	
	Came with free 'Dream Date' dress and 'Eiffel Tower' charm.	1967 to 1969
9GPS	Patch Doll in 'Dungarees' 1968 with 'Lucky Boot' charm.	
12GSV	Vicki Doll in 'Pink/Mauve Flared Mini Dress'	
	Came with 'Tennis Racket' charm.	1968 to 1971.
9GPP	Poppet Doll with Urchin haircut, wearing red jumper and tartan skirt.	
	Came with 'Double Heart' charm.	1968 to 1971

[New for 1968: a Golden Charm Bracelet with Sindy Medallion attached in every Sindy doll box.]

12SS1	Sindy Doll in 'Fashion Girl'	1968
12SS2	Sindy Doll in 'Beach Time Girl'	1968
12SS3	Sindy Doll in 'Ice Skater'	1968
12SS4	Sindy Doll in 'Miss Beautiful'	1968
12SS5	Sindy Doll in 'Evening Stroll'	1969
12SS6	Sindy Doll in 'Sunshine Girl'	1969
12SS7	Sindy Doll in 'Winter Warm'	1969
12SWM	Sindy Doll with 'High Fly Play Pack' extra outfits	1969
12WS	Walking Sindy Doll wearing navy and red dot suit.	
	Came with yellow coat-dress and charm bracelet.	1969
9PM	Patch Doll 'Dungarees' with 'Party and Play Pack' extra outfits	1969
9GPS1	Patch Doll in 'Blue Nightie'. Came with 'Lucky Boot' charm	1970 to 1972
9GPS2	Patch Doll in 'Patchpocket'. (For 1971/72 Patch had new bouncy hairstyle.)	1970
12WS1	Walking Sindy Doll wearing yellow jumper and mini skirt. Came with floral	
	coat-dress and charm bracelet.	1970/73
12SS8	Sindy Doll in 'Mini Skirt' 1970	
12SS9	Sindy Doll in 'Outdoor Girl' 1970	
9GPP1	Poppet Doll with long, straight fringed hairstyle, wearing striped coat-dress.	
	Came with 'Double Heart' charm.	1971/72
12SS10	Sindy Doll in 'Fun Furs'	1971
12SS11	Sindy Doll in 'Miss Sindy'	1971
12SS12	Sindy Doll in 'New Fashion Girl'	1971
12SS13	Sindy Doll in 'Midi Look'	1971
12SS14	Sindy Doll in 'Day Girl'	1971

12LS	'Lovely Lively Sindy' wearing pink patterned jumpsuit	1971/72
12LSC	'Lovely Lively Sindy' wearing 'Hearts Delight	1972
12LS1	'Lovely Lively Sindy' wearing 'Party Time'	1972
12SS15	Sindy Doll in 'Hot-pants' 1972	
12SS16	Sindy Doll in 'Pinafore Dress' 1972	
12SS17	Sindy Doll in 'Trendy Girl' 1972	
12SS18	Sindy Doll in 'New Day Girl' 1972	
12SS19	Sindy Doll in 'Sleep Tight' 1972	
FREE	June Doll wearing nylon panties (on redemption of 24 Heart Tokens). Three different June dolls: 9" brown hair early 1972; 11 3/4" blonde late 1972; 11 3/4" Fair '73.	

[By the end of 1972, all the charms and the Sindy 'Medallion Bracelet' had been phased out.]

S603	'Lovely Lively Sindy' wearing 'Classic Dress'	1973
S6055	'Lovely Lively Sindy' wearing 'Fun Flares'	1973
S606	'Lovely Lively Sindy' wearing 'Ship Ahoy'	1974
S653	'Active Sindy' wearing lilac tutu	1974
S651	'Top Pop Sindy'	1973
S604	'Super Sound Sindy'	1973
S676	'Fun Time Sindy'	1973
S633	'Sindy Apple'	1973
S213	Sindy 'Bride'	1973

SINDY OUTFITS FROM 1963 TO 1973

The outfits were also renumbered in line with the dolls and boxed sets.
Most outfits included shoes and accessories.

12GSS	Sindy doll in 'Weekenders' red, bue and white striped jersey and jeans.	1963/67
12SO1	'Sleepytime' pink and white checked baby-doll pyjamas.	1963
12SO2	'Undie World' French-navy bra, pants and slip.	1963
12SO3	'Dream Date' dark-pink cotton party dress.	1963
12SO4	'Lunch Date' moss-green polo jumper, tartan skirt and scarf.	1963
12SO5	'Skating Girl' red tights and circular skirt, red and white striped top and hat.	1963
12SO6	'Shopping in the Rain' black plastic mac, scarf and bag, red boots.	1963
12SO7	'Pony Club' checked shirt, brown jacket, beige breeches and hard hat.	1963
12SO8	'Country Walk' suede jacket, green jumper, brown plaid wool skirt (which was available in two different checks) and a dog on a lead called 'Ringo'.	1963
12SO9	'Bridesmaid' long lemon-yellow lawn/chiffon dress and bolero.	1964
12S10	'Seaside Sweetheart' orange checked shorts and top, towelling wrap.	1964
12S11	'Winter Holiday' white jumper, blue quilted anorak, red skit pants.	1964
12S12	'Emergency Ward' blue and white striped student nurse's uniform.	1964
12S13	'Happy Traveller' grey lightweight wool coat, suitcase and camera.	1965
12S14	'Air Hostess' blue gabardine uniform, hat and shoulder bag.	1965
12S15	'Centre Court' white 'S' monogrammed tennis dress and jacket.	1965

12S16	'Bowling' red T-shirt, white cardigan and beige cord Bermuda shorts	1965
12S17	'Evening Dress' long floaty evening dress, beaded bodice and stole.	1965
12S18	'Skirt Suit' two-piece skirt suit.	1965
12S19	'Trouser Suit' mustard cord trouser suit.	1966
12S20	'Cordon Bleu' navy blue and white striped apron and oven gloves.	1966
12S21	'Sail Away' yellow P.V.C. jacket, oilskins and sou'wester.	1966
12S22	'Care-free Camping' scarlet windcheater, white shorts and cap.	1966
12S23	'Come Dancing' blue and white satin strapless ballgown and stole.	1967
12S24	'Fur Fashion' black wool fur trimmed hat, coat and umbrella.	1967
12S25	'Housework' drill trousers and blouse with gingham pockets and pinnie.	1967
12S26	'Rainy Day' red and yellow coat, sou'wester, Bermuda shorts and red boots.	1967
12S27	Not issued.	
12S28	Not issued.	
12S29	'White Winter' white fun-fur coat, Cossack hat and Russian boots.	1967
12S30	Not issued.	
12S31	'Town and Country' trouser suit with skirt, shoes and boots.	1967
12S32	Not issued.	
12S33	'Belle of the Ball' long evening gown and stole.	1971
12S34	Not issued.	
12S35	'Discotheque' pink mini dress and lacy sleeveless jacket.	1971
12S36	'Sweet Dreams' pink nylon nightie, negligee and cap.	1971
12S37	'College Girl' yellow and mauve striped mini dress, hat and socks.	1971
12S38	'Disco Party' two-toned pink striped jumpsuit, bag and headband.	1971
12S39	'Shiny Shopper' red P.V.C. mini coat, scarf hat, tights and boots.	1971
12S40	'Bridesmaid' pink and lilac long, floral lace-trimmed dress.	1971
12S41	'Happy Holidays' tangerine striped mini dress and bag.	1971
12S42	'Weekend' rose pink bell-bottom trouser suit and black bag.	1971
12S43	'Skater' white fur-trimmed red skating dress, hat, scarf and mittens.	1971
12S44	'Look Warm' bright green or maroon trouser suit and scarf.	1971
12S45	'Winter Sports' yellow ski suit with rust brown nylon fur trim.	1971
12S46	'Midi Winter' brown tweed, chocolate fur-trimmed midi coat and hat.	1971
12S47	'Queen of the Ball' yellow long dress and scarlet coat with ric-rac trim.	1971
12S48	'Red Hot' mini dress and coat in red and white check red revers.	1972
12S49	'Blazer Way' yellow blazer, red and yellow check trousers and hat.	1972
12S50	Not issued.	
12GSS10	'Fun Furs' white fur coat, hat and boots.	1972
12GS11	'Miss Sindy' pink and blue horizontal striped long dress.	1972
12GS12	Not issued.	
12GS13	'Midi Look' multi floral midi-dress with long sleeves.	1972
12GS14	Not issued.	
12GS15	Not issued.	
12GS16	'Fashion Girl' floral pink and yellow pinafore, yellow T-shirt.	1972
12GS17	'Trendy Girl' striped red and yellow knitted jumper, red slacks.	1972
12GS18	'Day Girl' red mini dress with white bias trim detail.	1972

Also renumbered in 1973.

Even these pocket-money items included little coat hangers, shoes or accessories.

12S51	'Leather Looker' red skirt with braces.	1963
12S52	'Nylons' two pairs, one black one tan.	1963
12S53	'Sloppy Joe' red V-neck pullover.	1963
12S54	'Windy Day' blue beret and red pom-pom, scarf and muff.	1963
12S55	'Summery Days' orange multi check cotton dress.	1963
12S56	'Out and About' red and white check shirt red V-neck jerkin.	1963
12S57	'Cape' black and white hounds-tooth checked cape.	1963
12S58	'Duffle Coat' in tan felt with toggles, pockets and hood.	1963
12S59	'Springtime' printed cotton long sleeve blouse multi.	1964
12S60	'Sweet Swimmer' royal blue jersey swimsuit.	1964
12S61	'Coffee Party' knitted sweater dress in brown or blue.	1964
12S62	'Frosty Nights' red flannelette pyjamas.	1964
12S63	'Sindy's Hair Switch' available in three colours.	1965
12S64	'Cosy Nights' red flannel dressing gown.	1965
12S65	'Casual Moments' green turtle-neck sweater.	1965
12S66	'Summer Walks' pink linen skirt and crew-neck jumper.	1965
12S67	'Bra and Pants' white lace nylon set.	1965
12S68	'Shoe Set' the original shoes.	1965
12S69	'Summery Days' new multi check cotton shift dress.	1966
12S70	'Leather Looker' new black skirt and white jumper.	1966
12S71	'Smock Dress' green cord dress with smocking detail.	1966
12S72	'Bell Bottoms' white jeans with red stitching.	1966
12S73	'Reefer Jacket' nautical navy blue with brass buttons.	1966
12S74	'Tee Shirt' with 'S' detail.	1966
12S75	'Highland Lass' kilt skirt.	1966
12S76	'Denim underwear' mauve denim with checked waist-slip.	1966
12S77	'Cocktail Time' blue and black or green and black lace tiered dress.	1966
12S78	'Coloured Stockings' lace stockings in black and white.	1967
12S79	'Winter Undies' royal-blue long pantaloon undies.	1967
12S80	'Casual Frock' purple shift and pink hem gold buckle.	1967
12S81	'Hat, Bag and Shoes' turquoise hat, white bag, black shoes.	
12S82	Not issued.	
12S83	Not issued.	
12S84	Not issued.	
12S85	'Two tone Frock' pink and tangerine squared frock.	1968
12S86	'Pack A' record player, records, coke bottles, pin-up 'Dollybeats' picture, white shoes, pearl necklace.	1968
12S87	'Pack B' sandals, toilet bags and accessories, zip-up bag, brush comb, toothbrush and toothpaste.	1968
12S88	'Career Girl' pink and yellow polka-dot mini dress with white cuffs.	1968
12S89	'Mini Gear' blue suede mini-skirt and black jumper.	1968
12S90	Not issued.	
12S91	Not issued.	
12S92	'Flower Frillies' multi-print nylon bra, pants and slip.	1969
12S93	'Bedtime Beauty' blue spotted lavender nylon top and pants.	1969

12S94	'Trendsetter' multi-print dress, polo necked with bold buckle.	1969
12S95	'Cat Suit' purple nylon all in one suit.	1970
12S96	'Winter Coat' dark blue mini-coat with white saddle stitching.	1970
12S97	'Day Dress' pink floral top and plain pink skirt mini dress.	1970
12S98	'Day Girl' red mini dress with white bias trim detail.	1971
12S99	'Tights' white rib tights.	1971
12S100	'Floral Dress' multi floral daisy patterned mini dress.	1971
12S101	'Jodpurs and Sweater' red breeches and white sweater.	1971
12S102	'Midi Coat' turquoise and beige with epaulettes and belt.	1971
12S103	'Midi and Blouse' long red skirt and floral blouse.	1971
12S104	Not issued.	
12S105	'Casual Cords' blue cord flared trousers.	1971
12S106	'Blouse' long patterned over blouse.	
12S107	'Blouse and Belt' long patterned over blouse and belt.	1971
12S108	'Tangerine Dress' very short mini with floral scarf.	1971
12S109	'Poncho' red tartan with yellow fringing.	1971
12S110	'Hot-pants' turquoise bibbed with floral blouse.	1972
12S111	'New Dungarees' pink with white motif on bib and pink-check blouse.	1972
12S112	'New Puff Sleeves' patterned pink and purple dress.	1972
12S113	'Midi Look' navy and white daisy print midi-dress.	1972
12S114	'Cosy Coat' navy P.V.C. hooded coat with white fur trim.	1972
12S115	'Summer Party' lavender long dress, leg-of-mutton sleeves.	1972
12S116	'Fashion Girl' floral patterned pinafore and yellow T-shirt.	1972
12S117	'Trendy Girl' striped red and yellow knit jumper and red flares.	1972
12S118	'Blouse and Smock' blue and pink dress and white blouse.	1972
12S119	'Blazer' double-breasted navy and gold stripes with wide revers.	1972
12S120	'Mod Suit' midi orange suit, patterned blouse and scarf.	1972
12S121	Not issued.	
12S122	'Goucho' blue cord culottes and white shirt.	1972
12S123	'Bib Skirt' yellow bib skirt and blue-check blouse.	1973
12S124	'Lounger' turquoise and pink long dress with pink bodice trimmed with lace.	1973
12S125	'Sunbeam' red square-necked dress with bell sleeves.	1973
12S126	'Springtime' green and pink floral dress with puffed sleeves.	1973
12S127	to 12S199 not issued.	
12S200	'New Mod Suit' as before. Re-issued under new number as 'New Mod suit'.	1973
12S201	Not issued.	
12S202	Not issued.	
12S203	'New Summer Party' as before. Ditto as 'New Summer Party'.	1973
12S204	'Pop Show' flares and top.	1973
12S205	'Startime' floral pink long dress with fishtail hem.	1973
12S206	'Elizabethan' patterned long dress and scarlet cape.	1973
12S207	'Miss Beautiful' brocade long evening gown and velvet cape.	1973
12S208	'Pinny Party' long floral dress, yellow broderie anglaise over pinny.	1973
12S209	'Bridesmaid' long blue floral lace trimmed dress.	1973
12S210	'Zinga Ding' yellow blouse, scarlet and blue bell-bottoms, waistcoat and cap.	1973
12S211	'Theatre Time' pink and orange floral evening dress with dark-pink long over blouse.	1973
12S212	'Checker Decker' blue and white checked mini-skirt, waistcoat, blouse and tie.	1973

Also renumbered in mid 1973.

12SA1	'Sindy's Car' red MGB sports car.	1964/69
12SA2	'Sindy's Wardrobe' white with legs.	1964
12SA2/0	'Wardrobe' with outfits and shoes.	1967
12SA3	'Sindy's Bed' white 'Hollywood' headboard.	1965
12SA3/0	'Sindy's Bed' with dressing-gown outfit.	1968
12SA4	'Sindy's Horse, Peanuts'.	1966
12SA5	'Dressing Table and Stool' white.	1967
12SA5/0	'Dressing Table and Stool' with outfit.	1968
12SA6	'Bedside Table and Lamp' white.	1967
12SA7	'Camping Set' tent and sleeping bag.	1968
12SA8	'Washday Set' bowl, airer, pegs, iron etc.	1968
12SA9	'Sindy's Record' of Cliff Warwick and the Dollybeats.	1965
12SA10	'Sindy's Hair Colouring Set' colour sticks, curlers and shampoo.	1966
12SA11	'Sindy's Sink' bowl and accessories.	1967
12SA12	'Sindy's Bath Unit' bag, cap and towel.	1967
12SA13	'Carry-me-Case' dark pink with square, black handle.	1967/68
12SA14	'Sindy's Wardrobe Trunk' blue with drawer, shoes and dress.	1968
12SA15	'Chest of Drawers' white.	1968
12SA16	'Kitchen Table and Chairs' blue.	1969
12SA17	'Bell Chime Piano' white, worked with battery.	1969
12SA18	'Sink Unit'.	1969
12SA19	Not issued.	
12SA20	'Armchair' black and blue soft upholstery. (For one year only.)	1970
12SA21	'Easy Chair' black and blue soft upholstery. (For one year only.)	1970
12SA22	'Settee' black and blue soft upholstery. (For one year only.)	1970
12SA20W	'White Armchair' P.V.C.. (In 1972, this was available in a rusty-red P.V.C..)	1971
12SA21W	'White Easy Chair' P.V.C.. (In 1972, this was available in a rusty-red P.V.C..)	1971
12SA22W	'White Settee' P.V.C.. (In 1972, this was available in a rusty-red P.V.C..)	1971
12SA23	'Sindy's Town House'.	1970
12SA24	'Hairdryer' pink.	1971
12SA25	'Call and Talk Telephone'.	1972
12SA26	'Sindy's Super Show'.	1972
12SA27	'Dining Table and Four Chairs' laminated top.	1970
12SA28	'Sideboard'.	1971
12SA29	Not issued.	
12SA30	'Sindy's Buggy' vehicle.	1973
12SA31	Not issued.	
12SA32	'Sindy's Pack Flat House'.	1973
12SA33	Not issued.	
12SA34	Not issued.	
12SA35	Not issued.	
12SA36	'Sindy's New Pack Flat House'.	1974
12SA37	'Sindy's 7" Styling Head'.	1974
12SA38	'Sindy's Carry-me-Case' dark pink with round, black handle.	1974
12SA39	'Sindy's Pool Set'.	1974

PAUL OUTFITS FROM 1965 TO 1967

Most outfits included shoes/boots and accessories.

12MPS	Paul Doll in 'Casuals' blue jeans andred polo sweater.	1965/66
13MPS	Paul Doll with rooted hair in 'Casuals'. (For one year only.)	1967
13MO1	'And so to Bed' blue and white striped pyjamas.	1965
12MO2	'Seaside' red denim shorts and top.	1965
13MO3	'London Look' pale blue shirt, navy wool suit and tie.	1965
13MO4	'Motorway Man' brown felt car coat, check trousers and jumper.	1965
13MO5	'Time Off' brown suede jacket, grey check shirt, twill trousers.	1965
13MO6	'Soccer' yellow shirt, blue shorts and socks.	1966
13MO7	'Winter Sports' red heavy knit jumper, blue stretch pants.	1966
13MO8	'Medical Student' white cotton suit, stethoscope and skeleton.	1966
13MO9	'Camping' tent, shorts and zip top.	1966
13M10	'Tennis Party' white top, shorts and racket.	1966
13M11	'Ship Ahoy' yellow oilskin trousers, jacket with toggles and sou'wester.	1966
13M12	Not issued.	
13M13	'After Eight' dinner jacket suit, evening shirt.	1966
13M14	'Brands Hatch' racing coat, trousers and helmet.	1966

PAUL SEPARATES FROM 1965 TO 1967

13M51	'T-Shirt' white with red printed 'P'.	1965
13M52	'Swimming Trunks' blue and black stripe.	1965
13M53	'Casual Jacket' mottle blue and black or red and black collarless.	1965
13M54	'Raincoat' navy 3/4 length raglan coat.	1965
13M55	'Windcheater' zip-up padded coat.	1966
13M56	'Cardigan' beige and brown knitted cardigan.	1966
13M57	'Shirt' green and beige check.	1966
13M58	'Blazer' navy with 'P' on pocket.	1966
13M59	'Flannels' grey trousers.	1966
13M60	'Overcoat' dark (navy or brown) knee length.	1966
13M61	'Hat' beige brimmed hat.	1966

PAUL ACCESSORIES

13MA1	'Scooter' white.	
	(After the demise of Paul this Scooter became a Sindy accessory.)	1966

Most outfits included shoes and accessories.

9GPS	'Patch Doll in Dungarees' denim dungarees with red and white gingham, blouse, patch on knee and headscarf.	1965/70
9GPS1	'Patch Doll in Blue Nightie' full length blue winceyette nightie. (This doll had the new bouncy hairstyle for 1971/72.)	1970/72
9GPS2	'Patch Doll in 'Patchpocket'' new, paler version of 'Dungarees'.	1970
9PM	'Patch Doll Party and Play Pack' included 'Dungarees' and 'Birthday Party'.	1969
9PO1	'Schooldays' brown school uniform with beret and satchel.	1965
0PO2	'Swan Lake' white satin and tulle tutu and ballet shoes.	1965
9P03	'Bedtime' blue nightie and white quilted dressing gown.	1965
0P04	'Birthday Party' black velvet dress and red velvet cape.	1965
9P05	'Sou'wester' yellow mac and sou'wester with black wellies. (Also made in blue in 1966.)	1965
9P06	'Brownie' Brownie uniform, dress, beret, yellow tie and whistle.	1966
9P07	'Red Riding Hood' white and red spotted dress, apron, red cloak and basket.	1966
9P08	'Water Wings', navy swimsuit, green towel, water wings.	1966
9P08	'Water Wings' navy swimsuit, green towel and water-wings.	1966
9P09	'Half Term', tartan skirt, red jumper, grey blazer.	1966
9P10	'Toboggan' blue hooded jacket, red tights, mittens, boots and toboggan.	1967
9P11	'Hockey' brown shorts brown and yellow jumper, white shirt, stick and ball.	1967
9P12	'Easter Parade' broderie anglaise dress and ribbon-trimmed hat with basket.	1967
9P13	Not issued.	
9P14	'Summer Special' rose patterned dress and hat, toning coat and handbag.	1967
9P15	Not issued.	
9P16	'Winter Time' cord coat with lace trim, fur hat, scarf and mittens.	1967

9P51	'Overcoat' blue winter coat.	1965
9P52	'Vest and Pants' white Airtex vest and pants.	1965
9P53	'Easy Life' black polo jumper and matching tights.	1965
9P54	'Home for the Day' dogtooth check smock.	1965
9P55	'Blouse' white cotton blouse with rouched lace trim.	1966
9P56	'Casual skirt' blue skirt.	1966
9P57	'Summer Dress' blue gingham smock dress.	1966
9P58	'Shoes' white and black.	1966
9P59	'Red tights' red wool tights.	1967
9P60	'Flannel Dress' red felt dress.	1967
9P61	'Summer Suit' pink and blue cotton suit.	1967
9P62	'Casual Shift' cotton shift with T-shaped floral trim.	1967
9P63	Not issued.	
9P64	Not issued.	
9P65	'Winter Dress' long-sleeved dress with dogtooth bib and sleeves.	1967

PATCH ACCESSORIES

9PA1	'Bicycle'.	1966
9PA2	'Tent'.	1966
9PA3	'Pony' called 'Pixie'.	1967

BETSY OUTFITS FROM 1967 TO 1969

6GBS	'Betsy Doll' in red cord dress with white lace trim.	1967/69
6GB01	'Sleeptight' lemon floral nightdress, blue brush, comb and mirror.	1967
6GB02	'Fun and Games' blue and white checked trousers, blue top and dog called 'Hector'.	1967
6GB03	'Party Time' frilly pink ribbon and tulle dress with matching bag.	1967

MAMSELLE GEAR GET-UPS FOR SINDY 1965 TO 1969

DR350	'Sugar and Spice' little poplin shift dress with lace trimmed yoke.
DR351	'Blue Beat' crisp poplin day dress.
DR352	'Gear Nightshirt' cotton nightie and matching briefs, lace trimmed.
DR353	'Cool Cat' floral high-waisted, chiffon sleeved party dress.
DR354	'Fan Club' T-shirt with 'S' monogram and denim hipster skirt.
DR355	'Crochet Look' winter party dress, crochet sleeves and yoke, with fob watch.
DR356	'Sindy's Salon' everything you'd need for a shampoo and set.
DR357	'Pop-Posy' gay floral print cotton and pique shift dress.
DR358	'Oranges and lemons' crisp two-tone poplin day dress trimmed in white.
DR359	'Sindy's Garden' flower pots, trough, compost and seeds to grow.
DR360	'Pop Accessories' shoes, boots, bags and scarves.
DR361	'Op Art' two-tone dress with pop Art printed skirt.
DR362	'In the Mood' rave dress trimmed with lace and ribbon and with a hair ribbon.
DR375	'Sunday Best' sailcloth suit trimmed in white with a white handbag.
DR376	'Ship Ahoy' sailcloth trousers, fisherman knit sweater and duffle bag.
DR377	'Miss Mod' semifitted fully lined plaid Coat and Cap with shoulder bag and boots.
DR378	'Hello Dolly' Roaring Twenties party dress, headband and long necklace.
DR379	'Gad Abouts' cord pinafore and medallion on chain belt, sweater and tights.
DR380	'Paris Date' going away ensemble, printed dress and hat and duster coat.
DR381	'Miss Sindy Beauty Queen' velvet bodice, glitter skirt, sash and coronet.
DR382	'Spring Sunday' matching jacket, skirt and printed blouse and handbag.
DR383	'All Aboard' gay drill bell-bottoms, string shirt, captain's hat and duffle bag.
DR384	'Wild Cat' leopard skin trimmed coat and fur hat, bag and boots.
DR385	Not issued.
DR386	'Miss Cortina' chequered fabric shift dress and hat with contrast trim.
DR387	'Bahama Bound' super beach dress with bikini, hat, sunglasses and sandals.
DR388	'April Showers' printed P.V.C. mac with hat and boots.
DR389	'Gear Hats' assorted hat styles – smart, straw, sun, pillbox and knitted.

DR450	'String Vest' white Airtex set with 'Motor Sport' mini magazine.
DR451	'Track Suit' cotton jersey all-in-one zipped front jumpsuit.
DR475	'Group Gear' check black and white suit, collarless jacket with guitar.
DR476	'Sunday Date' suit with collar and revers, striped shirt and tie.
DR477	'King of the Road' zip-up bomber jacket and leather trousers with crash helmet.

PATCH GEAR GET-UPS 1967

DR400	'Land of Nod' dainty rosebud print shortie pyjamas.
DR401	'Teacher's Pet' denim dress and sun hat.
DR402	'Winter Walk' coat and hat with velvet trim and a dog called 'Hector'.
DR403	'Happy Returns' party dress with velvet bodice, tea set and cake.
DR404	'Tomboy' yellow sailcloth trousers and multi-coloured jersey.
DR405	'Autumn Leaves' warm patterned pinafore dress and ribbed polo sweater.

Tina
Faerie Glen
$11\frac{1}{2}$"/29cm
no markings
Dates: 1965

Two Tinas modelling tennis outfits. On the left, a pleated skirt, blouse and jacket. On the right, a towelling tracksuit. Clothes have 'Faerie Glen' labels sewn on them.

TINA AND GIGI
(Faerie Glen, 1965 to mid-1970s)

Faerie Glen, a company based in Walthamstow, northeast London, is a name known to two generations of children because of its wonderful selection of dolls' clothes and accessories to fit all sizes from baby dolls to girl dolls and teenage dolls. The company first began producing outfits in 1964. Hundreds of different outfits were made to a very high standard with over sixty different teenage outfits made for their own doll called Tina, introduced in 1965. This doll was $11\frac{1}{2}$" /29cm tall with jointed limbs and rooted short bouncy hair in many shades. She had painted blue, brown or green, side-glancing eyes with lightly painted eye shadow and a passing likeness to the 1966 Sindy face. Many of the dolls were completely unmarked, while some were marked 'Tina' across the shoulders.

The beautiful clothes for this doll included sports wear, underwear, rainwear, day dresses, evening dresses, trendy trouser suits, coats and hats – in fact, all the popular Sixties and Seventies fashions.

By the early Seventies, Tina had been replaced by Gigi. Also $11\frac{1}{2}$" /29cm tall, but with a different face, Gigi was an altogether more glamorous doll. She, too, had several shades of rooted hair, but in a longer straighter style and her body was more poseable, with joints at her head, waist, shoulders, hips, knees and ankles and with soft bendable arms. Her painted blue or brown eyes were forwarded facing.

Outfits for Gigi were in sparkling, glamorous designs and favoured a shimmery evening trousers style. The doll herself was unmarked, and came in a cellophane-fronted box.

Tina
Faerie Glen
$11\frac{1}{2}$"/29cm
no markings
1965
These two Tinas are dressed for evening. On the left, in a pleated tiered short dress trimmed with silver braid. On the right an organdie and lace ballgown with stole. The clothes have 'Faerie Glen' labels.

Tina
Faerie Glen
$11\frac{1}{2}$"/29cm
no markings
1965
Unusual daytime fashions with a Seventies flared longline trouser suit on the right and neat multispot two-piece suit on the left. Both outfits are labelled.

Tina
Faerie Glen
$11\frac{1}{2}$"/29cm
no markings
1965
A typical Sixties day dress on the left with covered button detail, while on the right a seventies dress with flared sleeves and buckled belt.

Clockwise from right:

Gigi
Faerie Glen
11½"/29cm
no markings
Mid 70s
A long brown haired Gigi wearing a silver trouser ensemble standing in front of her box.

One of the many glamorous outfits made by Faerie Glen for 'Gigi' and other teen dolls between 10"/25.5cm and 12"/30cm tall.

Gigi
Faerie Glen
11½"/29cm
no markings
Mid 70s
A flexible teenage doll with painted eyes, long auburn rooted hair and glamorous sparkling outfit. She stands in front of her original box.

Tommy Gunn
Pedigree
$11\frac{1}{2}$"/29cm
no markings
Dates: 1966
Tommy Gunn in basic Combat Kit standing next to his original
box, with Equipment Manual and Instruction Manual. Notice his
dog tag which bears 'GUNN T' on one side and a six digit serial
number on the other.

TOMMY GUNN (Pedigree, 1966)

Tommy Gunn, a soldier doll for the boys, was introduced in 1966 to rival Palitoy's 'Action Man'. He was made from rigid vinyl with moulded brown hair, painted blue eyes and a slim face with slightly pointed features. He had seventeen poseable joints enabling him to move into any position – kneeling, crawling, charging, marching, throwing, sitting, drilling, climbing, shooting, etc. He was presented in a box, ready for battle wearing a basic combat uniform consisting of trousers, tunic, black boots, elastic gaiters and a helmet. His identity disc had 'Gunn, T.' on one side and a six digit serial number on the other. He carried a Sterling sub-machine gun. In his box were his 'Instruction Manual' and 'Equipment Manual'. He measured $11\frac{1}{2}$"/29cm tall and was unmarked.

Additional outfits were available and included: a 'Battle Pack': self-loading rifle, '58' pattern equipment, entrenching tool, groundsheet and camouflage netting; 'Paratroop Pack': parachute harness, Sterling sub-machine gun, camouflage smock, knife and sheath, shockproof helmet and two grenades; 'Trooping the Colour': bearskin, scarlet tunic, blue trousers, white rifle sling, boots and dress belt; 'Communications Pack': portable radio, field telephone, map in map case and binoculars; 'First Aid Pack': stretcher, crutch, satchel, arm band and plasma bottle; 'Commando Pack': dinghy and paddle, Sterling sub-machine gun, bayonet and scabbard, cap, comforter, two grenades and a compass; and 'All Round Defence Pack': barbed wire with two supports, two landmines, entrenching tool, six sandbags, camouflage netting and foliage.

Other individual items included: Sterling sub-machine gun; grenades and bayonet; self-loading rifle; steel helmet and foliage; paratroop beret and knife; Carl-Gustav rocket launcher; sleeping bag; bivouac; badge of rank and medal; sand-bags; and an entrenching tool. All these realistic-looking items were made of plastic or fabric.

There were also child-size dressing-up outfits, so the child could pretend to be a soldier like Tommy Gunn. With each doll or accessory-pack purchased the child could ask the retailer for a 'medal sheet' and when twenty cards (found in each pack purchased) were saved and stuck on the printed sheet, they could be sent off to the manufacturer and redeemed for a free Tommy Gunn figure. A 'Victory V Card' was worth £3 and, obtained at the toy store with multiple purchases, could be redeemed against further purchases or a Tommy Gunn figure.

Alas Tommy Gunn did not prove as popular as his rival 'Action Man' and he was withdrawn after little over a year in production. He was re-launched in the early Seventies under licence to Zodiac Toys with an almost identical body and updated flock-sprayed brown hair. This version of the doll was marked 'Made exclusively for Zodiac (Toys) Ltd. Made in Hong Kong' across the back. He, too, had a range of outfits and accessories made exclusively for him, and he, only survived for less than a year.

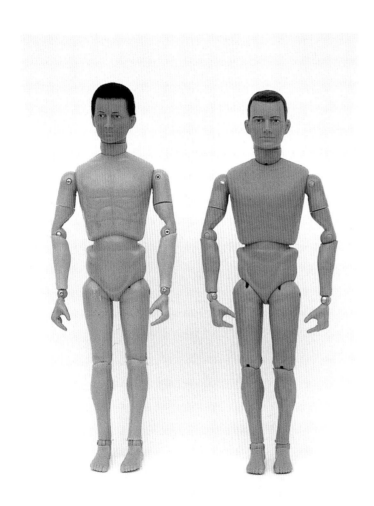

Tommy Gunn bubble packs showing 'Grenades and Bayonet' and 'Sandbags and Entrenching Tool'. Others included 'Sterling Sub-Machine Gun', 'Steel Helmet and Foliage', 'Self Loading Rifle', 'Paratroop Beret and Knife', 'Carl-Gustav Rocket Launcher', 'Sleeping Bag' and 'Badges of Rank and Medals'.

Naked Tommy Gunns. On the right, is a 1966 Pedigree Tommy Gunn showing his seventeen poseable joints. He is unmarked.
On the left a Tommy Gunn made under licence in the seventies for Zodiac Toys showing an almost identical body with the new flock sprayed brown hair. Both measure 11 ½"/29cm tall.
The Zodiac doll is marked Made exclusively for Zodiac (Toys) Ltd Made in Hong Kong.

Tommy Gunn
Pedigree
$11\frac{1}{2}$"/29cm
no markings
1966
Tommy Gunn All Round Defence Pack included barbed wire and supports, landmines, sandbags and camouflage netting.
Pictured with two Tommy Gunns in basic combat kit.

Tommy Gunn
Pedigree
$11\frac{1}{2}$"/29cm
no markings
1966
Tommy Gunn Field Communications Pack showing portable radio, telephone, map and map case with binoculars. Pictured with a Tommy Gunn in basic combat kit.

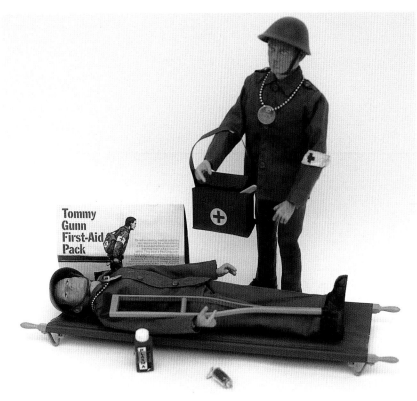

Left:
Tommy Gunn
Pedigree
11½"/29cm
no markings
1966
Tommy Gunn First Aid Pack showing stretcher, crutch, satchel, armband and plasma bottle. Pictured with two Tommy Gunns in basic combat kit.

Below:
This Tommy Gunn was made exclusively for Zodiac Toys under licence from Pedigree and is pictured with one of the bubble pack accessories and outfits also available for him in the early seventies. He measures 11½"/29cm tall and is marked Made exclusively for Zodiac (Toys) Ltd Made in Hong Kong across his back.

Left:
Tommy Gunn
Pedigree
11½"/29cm
no markings
1966
Tommy Gunn Paratrooper showing camouflage smock, shock proof helmet, Sterling sub-machine gun, knife, grenades, map and case.

Two Tommy Gunns escaping on a German Motorcycle Combination. Many companies made vehicles for these soldier dolls during the seventies.

COMPLETE LIST OF TOMMY GUNN ITEMS FOR 1966/67

11TGM	Tommy Gunn Solider Boxed	1966
11TG01	First Aid Pack	1966
11TG02	All Round Defence Pack	1966
11TG03	Field Communication Pack	1966
11TG04	Battle Pack	1966
11TG05	Commando Pack	1966
11TG06	Paratroop Pack	1966
11TG07	Trooping the Colour	1966
11TG08	Military Police	1967
11TG09	Cliff Assault	1967
11TG10	Marine	1967
11TG11	Bomb Disposal	1967

Super Packs

11TA1	Bivouac	1966
11TA2	Carl-Gustav Rocket Launcher	1966
11TA3	Mortar	1967
11TA4	Heavy Machine Gun	1967
11TA5	Rope Rocket Launcher	1967

Accessories

11TG51	Sandbags and Entrenching Tool	1966
11TG52	Steel Helmet and Foliage	1966
11TG53	Badges of Rank and Medals	1966
11TG54	Bayonet and Grenades	1966
11TG55	Paratroop written this way on manual Beret and Knife	1966
11TG56	Self-Loading Rifle	1966
11TG57	Sterling Sub-Machine Carbine	1966
11TG58	Sleeping Bag	1966
11TG59	Mess Kit	1967
11TG60	United Nations	1967
11TG61	Gas Mask	1967
11TG62	Poncho	1967
11TG63	R.A. Spott. Helmet	1967

Child-sized dressing-up clothes

TR60	Tommy Gunn Dress-Up Outfit Battle Kit	1967
TR61	Tommy Gunn Dress-Up Outfit Paratrooper	1967

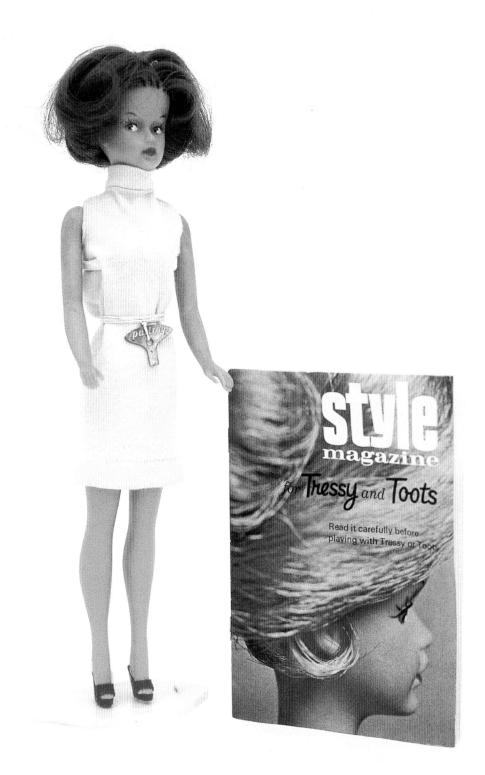

Tressy
Palitoy
12"/30.5cm
no markings
1964
Original Tressy illustrated with her Hair Styling Booklet, stand, cotton jersey sheath dress and metal key tied round her waist. This early Tressy had side glancing painted blue eyes and long straight legs.

TRESSY, MARY MAKE-UP AND TOOTS
(Palitoy 1964, 1965 and 1967)

'Tressy', little-sister 'Cricket' and Tressy's friend 'Mary Make-Up' were first introduced in the U.S.A. in 1963 by The American Character Doll Co. This company was one of the first to introduce vinyl teenage dolls – their 'Toni' and 'Sweet Sue' had preceded 'Barbie 1959' in the States. By 1964, Tressy had been introduced to Britain under licence by Palitoy – followed in 1965 by a little sister, called 'Toots' in the UK. Tressy's friend, 'Mary Make-Up', followed in 1967.

Tressy was the first of the Palitoy dolls to be advertised on television and was the first doll produced with a 'growing hair' feature. This mechanism consisted of a ratchet wheel within the doll's body around which was wound a long strand of hair that came out of the top of her head; the hair could be shortened by using a metal key inserted into the doll's back and lengthened by pressing a button in the doll's stomach. This unusual feature assured the doll a long life on the teenage doll scene, and she and updated variations ran for almost twenty years. Tressy was a 12"/30cm tall, slender doll made from rigid vinyl with only five movable joints (head, arms and legs) and with straight non-bending legs. She had painted side-glancing blue eyes and voluptuous red lips and came in one of three hair colours (blonde, auburn or brunette). Tressy was unmarked and came boxed in a cotton jersey sheath dress in a choice of lemon, turquoise or pink pastel colours, high heeled boots/shoes, a leaflet and stand for posing the doll, with her growing-hair 'key' tied at her waist.

Tressy's style was 'classic' rather than 'trendy'. The first doll came with all the appropriate accessories and, in 1964, her named, separately available packed outfits in were:

'In Holiday Mood': a jeans and striped top.
'Shaking the Night Away': a striped A-line shift.
'Evening Date': a frilled pale blue party shift with fur stole.
'Shopping in Town': a tweed suit trimmed in green.
'Winter Sporty': a Fair Isle jumper and ski pants.
'Leather Looker': a pink shift and red plastic leather-look coat.
'On the Beach': a blue swimsuit and wrap over skirt.
'Beauty Sleep': a pink nightie and negligee.
'Air Hostess': a navy two-piece suit, hat and bag.
'In the Office': a maroon pinafore with green jumper.
'Winter Journey': a black and white check coat with fur trim.
'Undie Fashion': a slip, bra and panties.

'Miss Fashion': a long, white evening dress, sash, bouquet and trophy.
'Hootenanny': a trousers, sloppy-Joe jumper and guitar.
'Blue Ribbon Winner': a tweed dress and brown bolero, rosette and dog.
'On Park Lane': a green swagger coat and hat.

Tressy had budget fashions, too, at pocket-money prices. These came presented in cellophane covered card and were also named. They included:
'Coffee Break': a green dress with wide white collar.
'Love Letters': a green velvet skirt and white broderie anglaise trimmed top.
'Special Date': a gingham shift with contrast yoke.
'Wild Enchantment': a blue and green shift.
'In my Solitude': a dark red shift.
'Soda Pop Cutie': a striped shift with plain blue bodice and white collar and button placket.
'Saturday Morning': a patterned trousers and trimmed white top.
'Walk in the Park': a blue patterned dress with white bodice and matching shoulder detail.
'Checkmates': a black and white shift dress.
'After Six': a black and white spotted shift.
'Summer Outing': a blue matching skirt and blouse.
'Lunching Out': a red skirt and top.

The clothing for Tressy was marked with a tiny embroidered label bearing the words 'Exclusive Tressy Empire Made'.

In 1965 a little sister was introduced for Tressy called Toots. This doll was smaller, just 9"/23cm and, unlike her older sister, had flexible limbs. She had the same 'growing hair' mechanism in three rooted hair colours (pale blonde, auburn and brown), painted side-glancing blue eyes and five movable joints. She was boxed wearing a white tutu, white pumps, a stand for posing her and a key for her growing hair mechanism. Like Tressy, she was unmarked. There was a lovely range of separately boxed fashion outfits available for Toots, including all the appropriate accessories, with such names as 'Schooldays' (white blouse and plaid pinafore), 'Yeah, Yeah, Yeah' (red flared dress with white collar), 'Fan Club Fan' (blue two-piece suit and white blouse), 'Hootenanny' (green circular skirt, red top and guitar), 'Kitchen Cutie' (green gingham dress and apron), 'Sugar-n-Spice' (pink party frock), 'Bowling Beauty' (red circular skirt and white blouse), 'Theatre Time' (dark pink lace trimmed shift), 'Happy Birthday' (lemon lace-trimmed party frock) and 'Winter Weekend' (Fair Isle jumper, ski pants and hat). Her pocket-money carded fashions included 'Pick of the Pops' (red skirt and denim top), 'Ship Ahoy' (red sailor top and white trousers), 'Poodle Parade' (blue check dress with two pet poodles on a lead), 'Party Time' (blue bodice and white skirted party dress), 'Little Painter' (red sailor-style dress), 'Garden Fete' (pink crossover bodice dress) and 'Undie Fashion' (white slip and panties). These garments were apparently unmarked.

Tressy's best friend Mary Make-Up was introduced in 1967 with a similar body to Tressy, but without the growing-hair feature. Instead, this doll had pale-blonde short, rooted hair that could be coloured or streaked with special water-based applicator sticks in fair, brunette or auburn shades and then easily shampooed out. Her eye lids, eyebrows, lips and nails could be painted, too, with the eye shadow, eyebrow pencil, lipstick and nail-polish supplied for her. A leaflet in her box showed the child what to do. Mary Make-Up was boxed dressed in a royal blue or red cotton striped shift dress, with sandals and a stand for posing her. The doll was unmarked and no specific outfits were made for her – her leaflet pointed out that Mary Make-Up was exactly the same size as Tressy and that they could share the same high-fashion clothes and accessories.

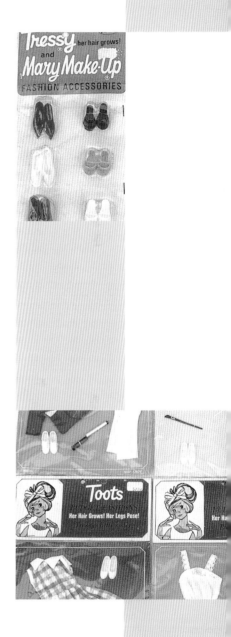

In the early Seventies, Tressy was updated – with an entirely new face, forward-facing painted blue eyes and three shades of hair (pale blonde, auburn and dark brown). The body and growing-hair mechanism remained the same and the doll was still unmarked. An entirely new range of clothes was available, too, including the dress in which the doll came – a long, V-necked lurex dress for a more glamorous style. Tressy's other new outfits included 'June Bride' (white wedding gown), 'Polka Princess' (long polka-dot skirted dress), 'Motoring Miss' (jumpsuit and jacket), 'Red, White & Blue' (blue dress with red and white striped trim and scarf), 'Regatta' (white top and trousers with sailor-style navy jacket), 'Trouser Suite' (denim blue top and trousers with cap, cream trimmed), 'Mix 'n Match' (skirts, trousers, tops etc in mix and match variations).

In 1979 Tressy was updated again, for the second and last time. She still had her growing-hair mechanism, but now had a moulded plastic key fixed to her back. The doll was operated in much the same way, with the key to shorten the hair and the release-button in her stomach to make it grow again. She now came only with blonde long glossy 'growing' hair, had a fuller face, painted forward-facing blue eyes and a smiling mouth. She also had a twist waist with flexible limbs and eight joints, including movable wrists and hands that could hold, a swivel head, legs and arms. She came dressed in a red or blue gingham skirt and plain matching red or blue gypsy style top and neat, matching heeled shoes. As well as the 'Mix 'n Match' and Seventies fashions that this Tressy could wear, a few more modern un-named outfits were added to her range, more in the style of the 'little housewife'. A few household items were introduced for her, too, such as an ironing board with iron, a cooker with pans, an upright vacuum cleaner based on an Electrolux model, and a smart supermarket shopping trolley. All these items were made of plastic and suggested that Tressy was now a housewife rather than the fashionable teenager she had been in the Sixties.

Toots was also updated in 1979, and was renamed Silky. She too had a fixed key in her back, slightly different hands and forward-facing eyes, but otherwise pretty much the same. She was now dressed in a red leather-look sailor-style suit or orange bell-bottom trousers with a multi-striped top. She came boxed under the Bradgate label, which was Palitoy's Wholesale Division, formed in 1971.

All the Tressy dolls were unmarked and the clothing from the Seventies seemed not to have the tiny Tressy label stitched into it, making the dolls and their clothing difficult to identify once out of their boxes. Tressy's 1964 box was triangular, with illustrations of the doll on two sides and a range of her fashions on the third. Late Seventies dolls had a cellophane-fronted box in keeping with current trends.

All these dolls were discontinued in the early Eighties.

Opposite, clockwise from top left:

Tressy
Palitoy
12"/30.5cm
no markings
1964
A pale blonde 1964 Tressy wearing the black and white tweed coat with black fur trim from 'Winter Journey'. Notice how the long hair strand comes out of the top of the head for styling in many different ways.

Tressy
Palitoy
12"/30.5cm
no markings
1964
Two 1964 Tressys. Left: auburn-haired doll wearing 'Shaking the Night Away'. Right: 'Soda Pop Cutie'.

Tressy
Palitoy
12"/30.5cm
no markings
1964
Two 1964 Tressys. Left: brown-haired doll wearing 'Leather Look'. Right: 'Walk in the Park'.

and here's *Tressy's* fabulous fashion parade!

Collect them all and you'll have the best-dressed doll in town. Look out for new additions to Tressy's wardrobe too.

From the Tressy 1964 Style and Fashion Booklet showing Tressy's fabulous fashion clothes and Tressy's Budget Fashions at pocket-money prices.

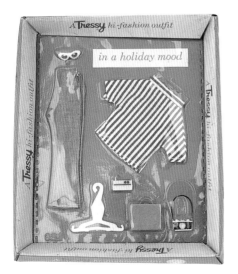

Top:
Four cellophane carded items for Tressy enabling the child to mix and match styles.

Above:
Tressy's cellophane carded tights and shoes pack. The tights pictured are heavy locknit and could not actually be worn with any of the dainty shoes made for Tressy.

One of Tressy's boxed outfits showing 'In Holiday Mood' and the reverse of the box showing more stunning outfits for Tressy.

Tressy and Toots are *pallitoy* dolls

Made under licence from American Character Inc
Broadway, New York

Cascelloid Division of
Bakelite Xylonite Limited,
Owen Street, Coalville,
Leicester, England

Bowling Beauty

Theatre Time

Happy Birthday

Winter Weekend

Top left:
Cellophane carded Toots fashions:
'Ship Ahoy', a sailor style top and trousers.
'Little Painter', a red dress and paints.
'Poodle Parade', a check dress with poodles.
'Undie Fashion', a white slip and panties.

Top right:
Four outfits from the 1964 booklet showing
Toots fashions.

Toots' budget outfits

Pick of the Pops
Ship Ahoy
Poodle Parade
Party Time
Little Painter
Garden Fete
Undie Fashion

collect these cute outfits for Toots

Schooldays

Yeah! Yeah! Yeah!

Fan Club Fun

Hootenanny

Kitchen Cutie

Sugar 'n' Spice

From the 1964 booklet Toots carded outfits at pocket-money prices on the left, and boxed items on
the right.

187

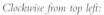

Clockwise from top left:

Toots
Palitoy
9"/23cm
no markings
1965
Toots standing next to her original box, wearing her white ballet outfit with metal key tied to her waist. The reverse of her box advertises many of the outfits available for her.

Toots
Palitoy
9"/23cm
no markings
1965
Auburn haired Toots wearing 'Happy Birthday'. Note the wrapped 'present', the cake and a 'pin the tail on the Donkey wallchart'.

Toots / Silky
Palitoy
9"/23cm
no markings
1965
On the right a fair haired Toots wearing 'Garden Fete'. On the left a fair-haired 1979 'Toots' with a fixed key in her back, slightly different hands, forward facing eyes, wearing a red sailor style suit. This doll was issued by the Palitoy Bradgate Wholesale Division and called 'Silky'.

Toots
Palitoy
9"/23cm
no markings
1965
The blonde Toots on the left wears 'Fan Club Fan', a blouse skirt and jacket with scrap book and pencil. The brunette on the right wears 'Hootenanny', a red top and green circular skirt with guitar and music sheet.

Mary Make-Up
Palitoy
12"/30.5cm
no markings
1967
Mary Make-up with her original instruction booklet, stand and clothing. These dolls were also available with a red dress. Applicator hair colour sticks and make-up sticks were provided with this doll, hence the name.

Mary Make-Up
Palitoy
12"/30.5cm
no markings
1967
Two Mary Make-up dolls showing the slightly different hair shade from different batches wearing Tressy Mix-n-Match outfits.

Tressy
Palitoy
12"/30.5cm
no markings
1972

Three new faced Tressys. From left to right: an auburn doll wearing a dark pink sheath, the brunette wearing Mix-n-Match Trousers and blouse, and a blonde doll wearing Mix-n-Match black gingham dress.

Tressy
Palitoy
12"/30.5cm
no markings
1972
An updated Tressy with a new face and forward facing blue painted eyes. Pictured with her booklet, cotton jersey sheath dress and metal key. In 1973 she was given a glamorous lurex sheath dress in three colours. A new range of fashions were introduced in the early seventies for this updated Tressy.

Tressy
Palitoy
12"/30.5cm
no markings
1972
Three 1972 Tressys showing three different hair colours. The outfits from left to right: 'Skirt and Blouse', 'June Bride', 'Trouser Suit'.

Tressy
Palitoy
12"/30.5cm
no markings
1972
A blonde Tressy with her hair strand wound out to waist level. She is wearing one of the new outfits 'Trouser Suit'.

Tressy
Palitoy
11½"/29cm
Palitoy on back of neck. All copyright reserved C.P.G. Products Corp Tressy ® Made in Hong Kong across shoulders.
1979
An updated Tressy 1979 standing next to her box with instruction leaflet and brush/comb. She came dressed in a red or blue gingham skirt and toning plain top. She had a new face, blonde growing hair with a fixed key in her back, gripping hands and a new flexible body.

Three cellophane carded Mix-n-Match outfits for Tressy which included jumpers, blouses, skirts, trousers, jackets and coats. 1972.

Three boxed New Tressy fashions from left: brown blouse with bib trousers; blue blouse and pinafore; and beige slacks and hooded jacket. 1972.

A boxed Tressy outfit depicting 'Regatta', a sailor jacket, bell bottom trousers, sweater, cap, bag and boots. 1972.